Shipwrecks & Seafaring Tales of Prince Edward Island

Shipwrecks & Seafaring Tales of Prince Edward Island

JULIE V. WATSON

HOUNSLOW

Nimbus Publishing Limited
PO Box 9166
Halifax, NS B3K 5M8
(902) 455-4286

Printed and bound in Canada

Canadian Cataloguing in Publication Data

Watson, Julie V., 1943-
Shipwrecks and seafaring tales of Prince Edward Island

ISBN 1-55109-368-5

1. Shipwrecks—Prince Edward Island—History 2. Seafaring life—Prince Edward Island—History. I. Title.

FC2611.W37 2001 971.7 C2001-900393-5
F1048.W38 2001

We acknowledge the financial support of the Government of Canada through the Book Publishing Industry Development Program (BPIDP) and the Canada Council for our publishing activities.

This book is for Ian Robson

who literally made it possible

when he tracked my computer virus,

saved what we could, helped calm my

nerves and made it all bearable.

Even as I retyped this book, I was

heartened by the knowledge that my

"computer wizard" was as close as the phone.

And for Nelda, who puts up with both

of us. And for Helen, who puts me up!

Contents (Major Items)

INTRODUCTION

ISLANDERS AND THE SEA

To understand and humanize the relationship of the Prince Edward Islander with the sea, it is best to look at the writings of those from an earlier era. One such narrative is by Malcolm A. MacQueen from his wonderful book *Skye Pioneers and "The Island."* This story goes back to 1803 when Lord Selkirk arrived with his first Canadian settlement of Highlanders who located in the area around Orwell. MacQueen wrote:

> *To every school boy the sea captain is a hero. In the fall of the year the docks were lined with ships loading cargoes of the famed McIntyre potatoes, or the equally famed black oats. The summit of the young boy's desire was gratified if permitted to bring a discarded whisky bottle full of milk to proffer the captain for the privilege of inspecting the hidden mysteries of the ocean Leviathan. Returning home, the assembled family heard of the wonders seen — the captain's cabin with its reeking lamp, the tiny sweating forecastle, and the cavernous hold in which was spied the dripping puncheon of Barbados molasses, nectar destined for the children's daily porridge.*
>
> *These sailors were courageous, stern men. Inured to hardship and facing dangers as their daily lot, they were disciplined and self-controlled. If, in a moment of dire peril, the mate's voice boomed above the fury of the storm, it was not a characteristic of the sailor. The same man, especially if a Highland Scot, was urbane ashore, speaking in that quiet undertone that is recognized as a characteristic peculiar to all sailors, and also one marking the speech of all the inhabitants of that beloved isle.*
>
> *For the first sixty of seventy years of the settlement's existence there were notable fishing grounds stocked with a plentiful supply of cod, herring and mackerel within a few miles of their homes. To these grounds the young men used frequently to go for a few weeks each summer. Erecting huts on St. Peter's Island they made it their headquarters, and did a thriving business with American shipowners who used to buy their catch. Unfortunately, these grounds no longer provide this source of pleasure and profit to the people.*

It is ironic that Mr. MacQueen was concerned about the decline in fish 180 years before the devastating fisheries crisis of the 1990s that has thrown Atlantic Canada into an economic turmoil, affecting the traditional lifestyle of a large segment of the population.

In yesteryear the sea provided a highway to the rest of the world. It was fraught with adventure, indeed with perils, yet it was the basis upon which commerce was built. For some it was simply a necessary means of getting to the Island — a settler for instance. For others sailing was a way of life, the sea as familiar as the fields and forests to a hunter. However tenuous or firm the relationship, no dwellers on Prince Edward Island, past or present, can ignore their dependence on the sea.

This book presents accountings of some shipwrecks and tales of life of the seafaring people of Prince Edward Island. By no means does it cover them all.

As I sit here typing this, the last thing to be done before sending my book off to the publisher, I want to rush down to the Provincial Archives for one more exploration of their files. But, I know Tony Hawke is sitting in his Toronto office, champing at my tardiness in getting the manuscript to him and eager to begin the process which takes it from my hands to yours.

My main hope at this juncture is that you enjoy the reading, as much as I have enjoyed the process of putting it all together.

Julie V. Watson

IN THE BEGINNING

Since we should leave the accountings of the Micmac race to their own historians, we begin our narrative about the land that was to become known as Prince Edward Island when Jacques Cartier is credited with "discovering" it in 1534.

George Edward Hart, a teacher of history at the Prince Street School in Charlottetown documented the event as he imagined it taking place. In his efforts to make history come alive for his students he wrote the book *The Story of Old Abegweit* in 1935. The natives gave the island the poetic name of Abegweit, meaning "cradled on the wave," though they sometimes called it The Island — Minegoo in their language — just as many of us do today.

1534

THE RIVER OF BOATS

It was a peaceful summer afternoon in old Abegweit. Beyond the red cliffs crowned with pine and cedar, was no stir of life except now and then the plaintive cooing of a turtle-dove or the cry of a caribou. As tranquil, too, were the waters of the bay below, broken only by the swish of paddles as a flotilla of birch-bark canoes sped for shore. In a few moments the Indians would have disappeared around the headland and so missed an unbelievable story to tell over and over again at the council fire. For over the bar and into the bay glided a longboat manned by many oarsmen. And sitting in the prow of the boat was a man whose piercing eyes and dauntless face told that here was a great Chief...

Their boat, their dress, their language was different and their skin was white — white as the moon-god when he smiled upon his people. Half in fear and half in wonder they started for their village, never stopping until they had reached the wigwam fires. There they told of the great white man whose face was as the noontide sun and of the others who paddled his huge canoes. Although the story was only half believed in the Indian camp, it was nevertheless true. The white oarsmen were the sailors of Jacques Cartier, and the chief was the great man himself.

His story is well known to all who have read Canada's tale of the past — how he set sail from Saint Malo, France, (April 20, 1534) with one hundred and twenty men in two small ships to look for golden Cathay, the realm of the Great Khan; how he reached a land quite different from China or Japan, but a land more precious than rubies in the hearts of the settlers who came long after him. In May, as Cartier sailed along the coast of Labrador, he said, "I think this is the land God gave to Cain." But when he had sailed farther south into the Gulf of Saint Lawrence he began to think that here was Cathay after all. He landed at a group of rocky isles which he called "Bird Islands" on account of the large flocks of gannets nesting there. He called also at the Magdalene Islands. On one of the little islands near the Magdalenes he first saw sea cows or walruses which he described as "great beasts like large oxen, which have two tusks in their heads like elephant's teeth and swim about in the water."

On June 30 he sighted our own island near East Point. For a whole day he skirted along the north shore seeking a harbour and in the afternoon reached the bay where he saw the flotilla of canoes. He gave this shallow water a beautiful name, Rivière des Barcques, or the River of Boats. This river must have been either Malpeque Bay near the entrance to the Narrows, or less probably, Cascumpeque Bay near the mouth of Kildare River. But he could not stop here because a shore wind arose and he had to turn his longboat back to the ship anchored outside the bar. All night long the intrepid explorer felt his way through a fog till, about ten o'clock in the morning, he sighted Cape Orleans, now Cape Kildare, and a little later North Point which he named "Cap des Sauvages." Cartier in an account of his discoveries related the following incident in connection with this point of land: "At this cape a man came in sight who ran along the coast after our longboats making frequent signs to us to return towards the said point. And seeing these signs we began to row toward him, but when he saw that we were returning he began to run away and to flee before us. We landed opposite to him and placed a knife and a woollen scarf on a branch; and then returned to our ships." So it was that a cape received a name ...

Rounding the Cape of Savages, Cartier sailed about ten leagues up the low-lying coast toward West Point. He was still looking for a sheltered roadstead when he came to the western entrance of Northumberland Strait. This opening which he called Saint Lunario Bay he thought was a great gulf so that, despairing of finding a haven in this part of the New World, he sailed north along the coast of New Brunswick. Thus it was that the French mariner sailed away with the belief that this realm "of delight, the fairest land that may possibly be seen" was part of the mainland. Jacques Cartier landed on our north-west shore on July 1st — a day which three hundred and thirty-three years later was to be known as Dominion Day. July the first, 1534 is a memorable date because on that day came the first white man to visit our coasts and leave a record of what he saw.

Can you not picture that tiny ship feeling her way north through uncharted waters, and, standing there in the stern, Cartier with his piercing eyes turned from the future for a brief instant to bid farewell to old Abegweit.

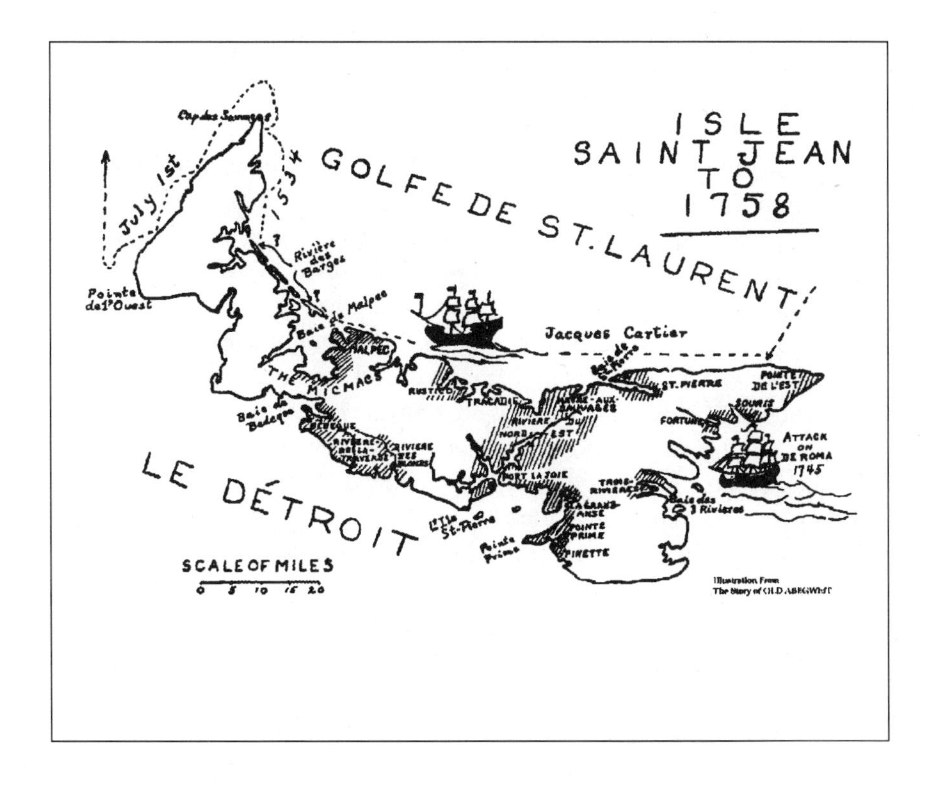

Illustration From
The Story of OLD ABEGWEIT

And so began an exciting nautical history of the land to become known as Prince Edward Island. And no such history would be complete without remembering the terrors that came by sea, as well as those wrought by its mighty force.

1745

BROUGHT DOWN BY NEW ENGLAND RAIDERS

Jean Paul DeRoma is credited with establishing what, for its time, was a model settlement in the area of Brudenell Point. Thirteen years had been spent planting and nourishing a colony on land granted by the King. The Frenchman was in fact the only one who had fulfilled his promises for the land, in spite of partners in France who tried to ruin his establishment and a plague of mice who ravaged a whole harvest ready for the sickle. So it was that DeRoma, sitting on the pier viewed the future as rosy in 1745. His people were contented with the luxury of working in a free land; his barns were full; his fishing and trading fleets were prosperous; and his acres yielded bounteous increase. There was something of June in the blood of DeRoma as he sat on the jetty dreaming. Never before in his whole life had he been so truly happy. His little hamlet would become the fairest land in the whole wide world so thought the father and founder of Three Rivers all-forgetting that the drama of a lifetime can be acted in a few brief minutes. Little DeRoma dreamed that, before sunset on that bright summer day, his settlement would receive a blow from which it would never recover.

Later in the day, a sail was sighted on the horizon. Monotony gave way to the bustle and excitement of preparation. But when the hospitable settlers discovered that it was an enemy cruiser, there was a different kind of excitement. What to do? There was a great hurrying and scurrying to and fro in the frightened colony which now resembled a disturbed ant-hill, while from the warship, anchored off the point, armed men rowed for shore. The French could offer no resistance for their total armament consisted of an old iron six-pounder fit only for saluting.

DeRoma, his son and daughter and five servants fled to the woods where they lay hidden. The New Englanders landed and ransacked every building. All articles of value were carried off to the ship. Nor were they satisfied with merely looting the place. They set fire to the buildings and soon the flames were leaping skywards. The episode broke the spirit of DeRoma. He and his family struggled through the wilderness for days until they reached St. Peter's, in "worn haggard condition." They took a ship for Quebec and never returned to their ill-fated colony at Three Rivers.

The sight of the settlement is marked with a monument which is still visited by many tourists. This was a minor incident in the War of the Austrian Succession, then raging in Europe but it was a sign of how the rivalry spread across the Atlantic. The American colonies, nurtured and tutored in strife, took up with zeal the centuries-old feud between Mother England and Dame France. The New Englanders, clamoured for the capture of Fort Louisbourg which had so long hampered inter-colonial trade in the North Atlantic. In 1745, Louisbourg was taken and an expedition was sent to destroy the principal settlements in Isle St. Jean. We just read what disastrous results attended the visit of this party to Three Rivers. Later Port LaJoie was the scene of the same kind of *warfare* — the equal combat between the hawk and the chicken. The Acadians, their homes in ashes, fled to the woods. The garrison of twenty men under Ensign Duvivier retreated up the Northeast (Hillsborough) River until, joined by a band of Micmacs and habitants, it turned and fought so fiercely that the enemy were obliged to take to their boats with a loss of nine killed or wounded. This skirmish was likely the only pitched battle between the English and French on Island soil. The French gave six hostages as a pledge of good behaviour and peace was made.

1749

CRYPTOGRAM, PIRATES AND BURIED GOLD

When the following story appeared in the July 1900 issue of *The Prince Edward Island Magazine,* it led to the publication of the "explanation" of a mystery a few months later. It does take time for this tale to get back to 1749, but eventually it does. It is this kind of revelation which could lead to scourges of treasure hunters digging up the earth. I've reprinted the whole document here in case there could be clues which will lead some reader today to untold wealth.

A LEGEND OF HOLLOW RIVER

Of the many tales of supernatural manifestations, connected with sequestered spots in P.E. Island, one of the most notable is, I think, that which I am about to relate. The place is situated alongside a small stream which empties into the Gulf of St. Lawrence and is known as Hollow River. A great many of the streams flowing into the Gulf should not have been called rivers at all, but creeks, as their supply of water is so small.

At one time, in the early history of this place, the public road was situated about ten chains from the coast. On one night somewhere about the year 1840, in the month of March, just before "Jack Frost" had withdrawn his command over land and sea, the ground on the slope towards the above mentioned stream and about one chain from the old road was taken out in two lots, exactly the size of two graves and placed on the ice which covered the steam. The pits were each about seven feet long, two feet and a half wide, and four feet deep. The most peculiar circumstances connected with the affair was that the soil which was dug out was deposited on the ice in compact blocks exactly the size of the pits, not a particle being loosened. A space of about one foot divided the pits. There were also three other pits marked, about the same dimensions in length and breadth but the soil had not been raised. The blocks which had been taken out held their form until the April thaw, then they lost their square shape and became mere piles of earth.

When the news of this wonderful event was made known, a great many visited the place and many were the remarks of wonder. It was considered no work of human power, but what or who did the deed remains a mystery to this day.

As events of curious happenings are sure to circulate in all directions, who chanced to hear of it but Donald Gordon. He at once came to see the place and thought that there must be gold buried underneath the dug pits. He, therefore, procured instruments for digging from the people living near at hand. He dug for some time till water came into the pit and he nearly perished. So he had to give up what he expected to prove a profitable discovery. It is not surprising that poor Donald Gordon failed in the discovery of gold, for although Klondyke was not at that time known, he did not undergo such hardships as some who have gone thither and with no better results.

When all wonder in reference to the occurrence had died away, the owner of the property, fearing that wandering animals might chance to fall into the pits, closed them up, so that at present day no one can tell the remarkable spot, unless he is accompanied by some of the oldest inhabitants of the place. Hence the reason this strange circumstance never was recorded anywhere.

At the time this affair happened few near the coast could either read or write — the same is true of other localities at that date — and as there was no attraction there for the sportsman or the angler, no visitor ever ascertained the old legend connected with Hollow River.

Senachie,
The Prince Edward Island Magazine
July 1900

AN EXPLANATION OF A MYSTERY

From the days of my youth old documents, journals, record, and all such relics of the earlier times have ever had for me the greatest fascination. Whenever I hear of the discovery of anything in this line that might be of special interest, I always make it a point to see the document, and if possible, to obtain possession of it. Failing this, I generally manage to obtain at least a copy. In this way I have accumulated in lapse of years quite a collection of manuscript, much of it interesting for its antiquity only, while a few of the papers are still valuable as having a direct bearing on some important questions which agitate the minds of some literary men even unto this age. To this latter class of writings in my possession belongs a copy of an old document found among the papers of a relative of a great-grandfather of mine — now deceased, peace to his ashes! — who, though not then feeling disposed to part with so interesting as heirloom, kindly permitted me to take from it a copy, according to my custom in such cases.

The document to which I now refer as having to do with a question still discussed among current topics in a certain locality relates to the origin of that apparently mysterious "phenomenon" which about sixty years ago caused such a furor among the denizens of Hollow River, and which, at a later date, has furnished Mr. Senachie with a skeleton for his "Legend" published in the ***Island Magazine*** *for July, 1900, and of which he asks if anyone can offer an explanation. In response, the "copy" to which I* *have referred is hereby respectfully submitted, not only for his enlightenment, but also for the perusal of whomsoever may think the matter worthy of their attention.*

Before giving my transcription I would detain the reader to say that the original of it bore every evidence of age and authenticity, and with the assurance of my friend of its genuiness added to this, I trust there may not be any great disposition to doubt the truth of what was recorded in so venerable a journal.

The original paper appears to be the remnant of a very comprehensive diary, and reads as follows:-

A.D. 1749, M. Sept., D. Sat. 2.

Some seasons by, while strolling along the shore at sunset, I espied glinting upon the water, some distance out from land, what appeared to me to be a large bottle, slowly moving shoreward. I turned about my steps in a direction to where I thought the floating glass would reach the sands, and there I seated myself upon a rock. After some short period of wait I was gratified to see it cast upon the beach but a few paces from the rock whereon I rested. In thinking this object a bottle I had judged aright, but it was not of such as size as it at first appeared to my vision. It was a vessel with a capacity of perhaps some half-dozen gills, but on picking it up, I found to my great surprise, that it contained nothing except a small piece of parchment closely folded, and sealed well with a seal. In the orifice of this bottle was placed a cork, and over this a seal was also placed a cork, and over this a seal was also placed, which I adjudged similar to the one placed upon the paper enclosed within.

The inscription upon this seal, then somewhat defaced by the action of the water, I was unable to understand, for the reasons that it consisted, besides some blossoms, of words writ in a language the which I do not possess the power to translate. I considered this language (as subsequently proved correct) to be of the French, for the reason that the letters resemble much the characters of our own alphabet, and furthermore, the words had a form in some instances, I thought, similar to those of the Garter on the Great Seal of His Majesty King George, imprinted on certain parchments the which I have seen. As I considered this curious parcel to be of some value, should I be able to ascertain its contents, I placed it beneath my cloak, and carried it home with me, so that I might examine it at leisure.

With some little difficulty I succeeded in removing the stopper with seal upon it, almost intact, the both of which I placed carefully away. With trembling hands I then drew forth the packet, on the which the seal proved to be, as I had conjectured, similar to the first. It was a note written, to my great astonishment, not even in the French, but in a number of consecutive unbroken lines, the which, at first sight, reminded me of the characters in an ancient book of the Greek, owned by my friend the schoolmaster.

On closer examination the letters proved to be of our own, but it was impossible to know their meaning, for the reason that they spelled no work. That my description may be better understood I copy the note below herewith:

eqEmegukOOokAIkE | mugOqE
jOkeuskAyqEmEoAY10, 1738 | kEAiMEyEusmAUeqAiE
g=l. l=3. A=A. | I. usio
eqIuOmEqfUAqcEceqeyO | gmokAmwmmOymImsEmcyq
EemugIosOOmAkkiUmuAmcsqEAuUqEJIccemkIm
eiuEEIigsuOmEgumcqgcAmcEkEnEmYewwouoAkk
usqgAo—kImEgAkckEmisgm.yEus eqOouOusgEme—o
IsuoIcckkEuEeOmc.ieqOyugAY.

Over this mysterious message, or whatsoever it may be termed I pondered and studied long. Every moment of my spare time I devoted to it, arranging in various forms the jumbled letters, with the hope that I might find a clue to their meaning — but all in vain. When I had despaired of solving the puzzle alone by myself, I showed it to all persons whom I considered likely capable of obtaining an idea of its contents. But all without success; none could understand any part of it, but what I plainly say myself, that is, what appears to be a date, the 10th day of a month, A.D. 1738. At length I began to suspect that I was being made the butt of some coxcomb's joke, and so my judging I soon thought little of what had so lately absorbed my thoughts.

But yesterday I had a visit from an old friend whom I have not seen for many seasons. He is the captain of a ship, and had many voyages to foreign parts.

Naturally our converse turned to things related to the seas, and the many curious incidents of a life upon the water. Suddenly I was reminded of my own curious find, and, as might be expected, I related the story of my long-forgotten bottle with its mysterious note. As a consequence I heard from my friend a story, romantic, it is true, but the which, notwithstanding, has increased greatly my interest and rendered me still more desirous of reading the secret message.

While on a voyage to the New-found-land and the islands of France in that quarter also, my friend the captain chanced to meet with, in the harbour of St. Pierre, a mariner who was about to cross the Ocean. This man, on learning that his new acquaintance came from the "Isle St. Jean," related him a wondrous story.

Born in the seaport town of Harve, he had at an early age taken to the sea. He had in early life he said, been possessed of an uncommon longing for adventure, and he was afforded abundant opportunity of indulging his desire in those turbulent times. After a short service in the navy, he deserted and went in search of more exciting work. A position which promised to satisfy him he soon found on a privateer, "The **Eagle,**" *then about to sail for America.*

This craft was under the command of a lawless being who acknowledged no overlord wither here or in the Hereafter. Indeed it appears that of the latter he never thought.

The real nature of his duties the young adventurer was not permitted to know until they had reached to a distance some days out from the land. Then he was startled to learn that the occupation of this vessel was to be of the nature indicated by its name — prey in upon others. He had, unwittingly, joined a band of pirates. He was placed in charge of the guns, of the which they had four on board. (To follow them through their various exploits after crossing the Ocean, would require more time than I can now spare.) Hovering about the Gulf not far out of the way of the vessels trading between the colonies and the mother countries, they obtained by force not only everything they needed, but their ruthless chief, by many a heartless deed, added continually to his store of booty. Soon they became the terror of all mariners trading in those waters. By their deeds many a stout ship was sent a helpless derelict over the waste of waters, and many a harmless sailor was given a watery grave. About a year passed over, and the young pirate began to having longings for some position more pleasing to his tastes. He wished to be put on shore, but of this the captain would not hear, for the double reason that his naval training served him well in the handling of the cannon, and moreover that he feared a report of their proceedings might by this means be spread abroad, and the names of all be known. But Providence came to the rescue. Early in the summer of the year 1738, the buccaneers fell in with a brig bound for the British colony of Massachusetts. The ship escaped without serious injury being inflicted upon her by the armed ***"Eagle,"*** *but they were obliged to leave behind as a prisoner in the hands of the pirate one who had proved to be over zealous in the defence of his ship.*

Once taken on board, this unfortunate was courteously relieved of everything in his possession, and though constantly watched by his captors, was then allowed the liberty of the ship. Furthermore, as the youngest of the crew (the man from Havre) discovered to the prisoner more feeling than was pleasing to the master, he was, as a means of rebuke, to be held responsible for the safe-keeping of the object of his commiseration.

Among other articles found in the possession of their captive, was a fragment of a paper published in the city of London. Although in English, its contents was readily known to the captain, for the reasons that he was learned in both languages. This qualification was possessed by the English captive also, although he very wisely took care not to disclose any knowledge whatever of the French. One thing in this paper that greatly interested and soon alarmed the captain was a proclamation of the king offering a reward of several hundreds of pounds for the capture of the very vessels the which he now commanded. He learned from the captive, with whom he conversed freely in the English, that the proclamation had only recently been issued, but that even then, several armed craft were on their way to the Western waters, all confident of obtaining the promised prize.

To flee with their treasure would be useless; defence with four small guns was impossible. A consultation was therefore held, and the course of action deemed most expedient was soon decided upon.

The captive, though always closely watched, was not prevented from being within ear-shot of the others as they formed their plans; the captain, as appeared strange, never seeming to suspect that he might understand what converse was being made.

What the crew had decided to do might easily be guessed. Their intention was to hide the guns and treasure on the land in some secluded spot, where they might return when all search for them had ceased. Once rid of their guns, and having on board no thing that was not necessary for all mariners commonly, they could never be suspected of being the breakers of the law.

The **Eagle**, *having proceeded rapidly to the north until they passed the east cape of this island on their left. Then they steered to the west, close along the northern shore until they arrived at a position neighbouring to a settlement of the Acadians on the shores of a pond of goodly size. Here the captain, with one man, went upon the shore. Next evening they returned, bringing with them a number of the implements used by the farmers in cultivating their land, and also in erecting the dykes upon the banks of the ponds.*

The captain then gave orders to proceed outward from the land. At nightfall they again steered to the west, approaching gradually to the shore until at a distance some few miles west of the settlement they were as close to the land as it was possible to come, without having their ship upon the sands.

Here a small stream flowed into the sea, and along the banks was a luxuriant growth of bushes. Here they cast anchor, and the captain, with all his followers but one, went with their goods upon the shore. One was left, the young adventurer from Havre (who told my friend this story). To his great chagrin he was entrusted to mind, and guard from escape, the Englishman. Anxiously did he follow with his eyes his comrades as they proceeded to the land, but they were soon lost to his vision in the gloom of the shore. Still did he gaze after them, paying little attention to his cargo, who now wandered at will through all parts of the ship, and troubled his guard only to ask of him a flask of the wine with which his floating prison was well supplied.

But the plan of the men upon land I had almost forgotten to record in this account of my friend's narrative. Even near Louisburg, before entering the strait, they had commenced their work. As it was their intention to bury in the earth their treasure, they very naturally thought necessary to have it, and the guns, enclosed in some manner so that they might not only be placed more easily in their hiding place, but also more conveniently removed at the earliest opportunity. They therefore, set to work to make boxes of wood in which the guns would fit closely (one gun in each box). This, as one familiar with the shape of a cannon-barrel knows, would give the boxes much the appearance of a coffin, wider towards the breech, and becoming smaller towards the muzzle end.

For the treasure no other packages was necessary than those which held the guns also, for the simple reason that, while the guns were round, the boxes enclosing them were necessarily of a square shape, so that a sufficient space would be vacant in the four boxes, both in and outside the guns, to hold all the treasure that they wished to place away. (This may readily be seen by taking a copper piece and placing about it a square, sufficiently to enclose it.) To dig pits and cover up the boxes would be simple work. But they intended to return as some future time, and take away what they were now placing here for safety. When everything was packed in the boxes, and the covers closed, they began to devise some means whereby the future work of unearthing might be most easily done. Soon they agreed upon a plan. Additionally boxes to the number of four were soon constructed, of exactly the same length and breadth of the smaller ones. They were about four feet in depth and without covering. Their use was to be this. When the pits would be dug about six feet in depth (that is exactly the added depths of a large box and a small one) the small and valuable boxes were to be placed on the bottoms, and down over them the large and empty ones be lowered. Into the open boxes on the top the earth removed from the pits was to be returned, and the turfs then carefully placed in a position so as to conceal that they had ever been disturbed.

By this arrangement all that would be necessary in moving the treasure again would be to raise the upper box of earth instead of digging through the four feet of clay.

Now after an absence of several hours, (hours of hard working for the one party, and of anxious waiting for the other) the men returned to the ship. Everything that might give the ***Eagle*** *an appearance different to trading vessels was either thrown overboard or concealed. Once more they set sail for the East — but to follow further is of no interest.*

The adventurer from the port of France was left, with the English sailor, at another seaport in his native land, and the ***Eagle*** *continued on her course down the Mediterranean. Some years after he had visited the Island of St. John, in hope of finding some trace of the treasure he had so well helped to obtain, but all his search was in vain. He had trusted to his memory to find the place, but was disappointed. He was then leaving St. Pierre to settle in the land of his birth.*

Such was my friend the Captain's story. Incredibly as it appears at first, it has set me a-thinking. May there not be some connection between it and my untranslated note? The year he says, was A.D. 1738; my note clearly shows the same number. The vessel was from France; the seal is of the French number. The mariner remembered of giving the prisoner a flask of wine; may not this be the very vessel in which the note was borne to my hands? The English Prisoner had abundant opportunity of preparing and sealing such a message, the which he might afterwards have lost or intentionally cast into the water.

My earnest hope is that, by favor of Providence, I may yet be enabled to understand this message, and, if not, that my heirs may not lose any interest in its contents, but strive as earnestly as I have done to obtain its meaning. If successful they may be rewarded with becoming possessors of all this hoarded and hidden treasure of the buccaneers from the shores of France.

This record with its "romantic tales" leaves little to be explained. That the money was buried at Hollow River, "a small stream a few miles west from a pond," etc., is quite evident. Were the cryptogram deciphered it might "Make assurance double sure," but this work the writer does not now intend to undertake. He leaves it to some indulgent reader blessed with more skill and patience than it is his fortune to possess.

Whether or not the meaning of the "mysterious message" be ever ascertained, we have in the other record — if true — a very satisfactory explanation of what gave rise to the ""Legend of Hollow River."

And what makes the account more interesting is that we have it all as a result of the contents of a bottle.

D.A.W.
"An Explanation of a Mystery"
The Prince Edward Island Magazine
October 1900

1751

A JOURNEY FROM PORT LA JOIE TO ST. PETERS

The following is not about a shipwreck, or even a really exciting adventure — although it probably seemed so for those involved. What it does is give us a picture of the Island in the early days of French settlement. We have only reprinted enough here to give a picture of Charlottetown Harbour as it was in 1751.

Colonel Franquet was an Officer of Engineers, and had been sent from France to superintend the new fortifications of Louisbourg, and devise a system of defense for the French possessions which lay in the Gulf of St. Lawrence. Carrying out the latter portion of his commission he visited the Island of St. John in 1751, and furnished a report with plans of the military works necessary to place the French colonies on the lower St. Lawrence in comparative security against sudden attack. Franquet, if we may judge from his report, was an officer of keen observations and excellent judgment. He does not confine himself to the dry details of planning redoubts and discussing the advantages of rival positions, but takes diligent note of the appearance of the country, its products and capabilities, the condition of the settlers and their prospects, and in this way bequeaths to us a valuable document which throws much light on the history of the Island at that time. To turn to the fullest advantage the information contained in this record, I have thought it well to follow the traveller down in his journey of work and observation, and set down the incidents and comments as they occur.

A fair wind had carried the vessel which bore Franquet from Louisbourg through the "Passage de Fronsac" — Canso — and round the lofty promontory of St. Louis, Cape George, but after passing Pictou Island, it shifted round to the northwest, and the thirty-first of July and first of August were spent in beating between the shores of Acadia and the Island. On the former he noticed the Harbour of Tatamagouche, which he was told lay only seven leagues from Port Lejoie. On the Island shores he passed Cap à L'Ours, and les Isles à Bois (Cape Bear and Wood Islands) and

Point Prim. On the third of August the wind was favourable and the vessel laid her course up what was then called the Great Bay of Port Lejoie. The hidden dangers caused by the reefs running out from St. Peter's and Governor's Island are mentioned, and pilots are cautioned not to drift from the channel.

At length they ran through the narrow entrance with Point a la Framboise on the right, and Point de la Croix, from which a huge cross rose high above the water, and onward still past Point de la Guerite, whence the watchful sentinel paused in his walk to note the passing craft, then under the graveyard, and on till opposite Point Marguerite, now Battery Point, on the southern shore, and the creek on the northern side formed by the small stream that runs to the sea through the valley of Warren Farm, when the vessel came to anchor. Franquet contemplated with delight the magnificent natural harbour that stretched out before him — its waters surrounded with a rose-coloured beading, set in an ebony frame of dark forests, that covered the red shores and extended up along the courses of the three great estuaries. Only on the rounded heights and shelving slopes of Port Lejoie had the monopoly of the fest been invaded. The houses of the settlers could be seen scattered along the sides of the valley, while the more pretentious buildings of the Government crowned the summit, and rose on the seaward breast of the emince that rises with a long gradual ascent from the landing creek towards the harbour's mouth. The romance of the scene was somewhat impaired by the discomforts to be encountered in landing. Only at high water could a boat approach the ridge that spanned the creek. At other times the boat's services had to be supplemented by wading along the flats in order to gain the shore.

by John Craven,
P.E.I. Magazine, September 1900

THE ACADIAN EXPULSION — AN ERA OF NEW HOPES; TRAGEDIES

When an event is recounted by more than one individual it will often change drastically in the telling. The perceptions of the storyteller flow over into the interpretation. In the case of the Expulsion of the Acadians from Isle St. Jean (as Prince Edward Island was then known) in 1758 these two writings offer two different perspectives. The second writer, J. Bambrick, was obviously fascinated by the events which took

Acadian settlers as far away as the Faulklands in the Southern Hemisphere. In his narrative, however, he completely ignored the fact that some 700 Acadians drowned when being forced from their Island homes. P. Blakely and M. Vernon (in the first extract) recounted the details of that event in their book, *The Story Of Prince Edward Island*

I must admit to wondering about the truth of both stories, so will leave the reader to decide which is the most accurate. Or perhaps, the truth lies between the two.

To set the scene: In 1755 the British had successfully expelled the French from Nova Scotia. It was the first foothold in what was to become a war to win control of America. Both England and France wanted the continent and were willing to fight for it. When the British captured Louisbourg in Cape Breton, the French also gave up Isle St. Jean.

Under the terms of the surrender, those French citizens currently living on Isle St. Jean were to be given the choice of returning to France, or swearing allegiance to the British. Lord Rollo, along with 500 soldiers and tradesmen, travelled to the Island which the British renamed St. John's Island to build Fort Amherst. Several French officers were also sent along by the Governor of Louisbourg to tell the French garrison and the people to lay down their arms.

Many refused to surrender, and they fled. Lord Rollo and his soldiers sought out as many as they could and loaded them onto the boats to return to France — an event that became known as the Expulsion. In the spring of 1759, when the British returned, the Acadians who remained were hiding and could not be found. About 300 remained on the Island and eventually took the Oath of Allegiance to the British King. These were the ancestors of the Acadians living in Prince Edward Island.

1758

THE LOSS OF THE *DUKE WILLIAM* AND THE *VIOLET*

In the fall of 1758 Lord Rollo's soldiers had about 3,500 people bound for France. They had with them clothing, bedding and some household effects and plenty of food and water were on board for the voyage.

The largest of the ships was the *Duke William* under the command of Captain Nicholls. The most important French settlers, including Abbé Girard the priest, were put on board her.

On November 25th seven ships sailed out of the Bay of Canso on the way to France with about 1,500 of the French and Acadian prisoners on board. **Duke William** *led the convoy which was hit by a sleet storm on the third day out from land. In the storm, which lasted for many hours, the ships became separated and it was not until December 10th that the outlook on* **Duke William** *sighted the* **Violet.** *This ship had suffered direly in the storm and was leaking badly; a situation worsened by choked pumps.*

Captain Nicholls shortened sail in order to stay close to the **Violet,***and promised to send over another pump as soon as the wind and seas calmed.*

While the two ships were sailing along, an immense wave hit the **Duke William** *so hard that the captain was knocked off the chair on which he was sitting smoking his pipe. In a few minutes the mate told him that there was water in the hold. Captain Nicholls and the carpenter went below, where they found water pouring in around a timber that had been knocked out. The crew tried to repair the damage, but in vain. Water kept rushing in. Captain Nicholls awakened the French and asked them to help with the pumps. They immediately got up and cheerfully assisted.*

When dawn came, the **Violet** *was lying broadside in the seas, while the crew were trying desperately to cut away a broken mast. Suddenly both ships were struck by a squall. When it cleared ten minutes later, the* **Violet** *had disappeared. Four hundred people were drowned in her.*

The water was still pouring into the **Duke William.** *The Acadian women used the wooden tubs they had brought on board for washing to empty water over the side of the ship. For three days the Acadians pumped and bailed steadily. On the fourth morning the French came to Captain Nicholls and said despairingly that it was useless to continue, as the vessel was full of water. Sadly the captain agreed and asked the priest to give his people absolution.*

There were only a few lifeboats on board, not nearly enough to save everyone. The crew prepared the lifeboats for launching, although the sea was too rough for small boats. Then one of the look-outs shouted that he saw two ships. The crew of the **Duke William** *hoisted the distress sinal and fired the ship's guns slowly to draw their attention. The two ships sailed away, probably because their captains thought the* **Duke William** *was an enemy warship. Another day, which was hazy, they saw a Danish ship, but she too sailed away.*

Some of the Acadians came to Captain Nicholls to say that they were prepared to die; they begged the captain and crew to save themselves, and to take the priest with them. After some hesitation, the captain followed their suggestions. Soon after the captain and thirty-five men had pulled away, four young Acadians found a jolly-boat on the ***Duke William****. They threw it and two paddles overboard, and swam out to the little boat. After they had climbed into it, they saw the* ***Duke William*** *sink. As she went down in the sea her decks blew up with a noise like a clap of thunder. About 300 Acadians on board were drowned. The men in the rowboats reached the English coast safely, and later the priest and the four young Acadians were sent to France.*

P. Blakely and M. Vernon
The Story of Prince Edward Island, 1963

1758

OCCUPATION OF EAST RIVER AND ST. PETER'S

This place and the other old town site at Savage Harbour have had many visits from "treasure seekers," who, sometimes, during the "wee sma' hours," dug extensive holes, often among the growing crops. This belief in buried treasure is also prevalent among the descendants of the Acadians — particularly those around Maisonette and Caraquette, N.B.

The line of travel at the time was along St. Peter's Bay to the head; thence a trail followed a valley or level country by Groshaut, and onto the head of the present Rollo Bay; where another extensive settlement existed.

During the wars between France and England, previous to 1758, Isle St. Jean had happily escaped any hostile visitation; but after the final capture of Louisburg and Isle Royale, the British made a descent on the Island. Gathering all the small craft that had been present at the siege of Louisburg, and some armed vessels with a considerable force under Lord Rollo, they came round Isle Royale, and entered the gulf; presenting an imposing sight as they neared Rollo Bay. To the terrified settlers the sea seemed covered with white sails; and they counted 300 in all. But most of them were small crafts; for every boat (from Nantucket to Terre Neuve) was impressed into the British service at the siege just ended.

As they prepared to land the Acadians gathered their families and most valuable effects, and fled by the trails to St. Peters thence to the "Capes of Savage Harbour," as tradition gives it. Here a council was held; and when the booming of cannon at Port La Joie told them that it was invested, and as scouts brought in word that the enemy was being guided along the trail by "Webster" (a name not in favor with them afterwards); they decided to bury their valuables. Their traditions also say that they, at this time, buried the church vessels and other valuables in a small brass cannon somewhere in the vicinity of the Church of the Hillsboro.

When they surrendered they were required to take the oath of allegiance to the British Crown, which many of them did not understand — thinking it contained something hostile to their religious belief.

After so many wars with England it was only natural that hard feelings should exist among the Acadians. So there was a desire among many of them to depart. Some hoped that Quebec was not permanently annexed, and as many had the means to do so, went thither — only to find Le Drapeau Britannique floating from the citadelle. They also became aware that they were not included in the surrender and very favourable terms of the Quebec Treaty.

The clergy advised them to return and accept the new order of things; and, with encouraging words, pointed out to them that "those who settled in the country would still own the country." Some did return, and one of them afterwards said: "we had to come back, and take off our hats."

Their descendants to-day have reason to bless this wise policy.

Those who remained in Quebec, or went elsewhere, account for only a few of the once numerous Acadian settlers of the places mentioned; yet to-day there is not a French name among the settlers of Hillsboro, Pisquid, Tracadie, French Village, St. Peter's or vicinity. I believe I have the key to the cause of such a general exodus as the Acadians from these parts. No doubt the proximity of a British garrison, at Port La Joie, induced some to depart to more secluded parts of the Island. They certainly disappeared within three or four years after the change of masters; for the new settlers, coming in fourteen years after the cession of the Island to Britain, found a thick, young growth of trees, as tall as a man, covering the old French clearings along the Hillsboro River.

Now, soon after the treaty of peace was made, the French Government fitted out an expedition of three ships, one of them an armed vessel, to carry away a number of Acadians with the consent of Britain, and plant a colony in the Malouine Islands.

I have seen the journal of the French Père who accompanied them to their new homes; but it did not state the particular place from which the Acadians were embarked. The expedition was under the command of Colonel Bougainville; under him were Captains Massie and Chanal; Lieutenants Huillier, Duclos, and De Gurayadaris.

With chivalric loyalty, worth of La Vendée, these simple-minded Acadians chose to follow the Lilies of France again; to endure the loss of property here, and to suffer the discomforts of a sea voyage, the length of the American continent, in order to found new homes. That most certainly was the age of sentiment; for some of those who came to replace them abandoned home, county and property, in the states, to live here under the British flag.

No doubt it cost the Acadians many a pain at leaving. The Island was a land of forests of almost tropical beauty which rose in maple-fringed terraces from the water's edge; the sparkling rivers fed by crystal springs and bordered by the light green intervals were teeming with fish and wild fowl. They had led picturesque lives among such scenes, but never again should the songs of Normandie be heard by the romantic banks of Morel; not the voice of Mathilde or Melanie, of a summer even, calling "Chow-Chow" from the homestead to lure the cattle home at milking time.

Again do I see in fancy the embarkation at Port La Joie, the procession of old and young and the white-kerchiefed maids of Brittany, who wave to Isle St. Jean an eternal farewell, and, like Marie Stewart, say: "Adieu, sweet land of France, Adieu."

Then for a few years silence reigned around the old homes, until a new people came from beyond the sea to fill their places. Meanwhile, how did the Acadian colonist fare?The ships met with a fierce storm near the mouth of the La Plata River, a regular "Pampero"; and they were obliged to call at Monte Video to refit.

This part of South America was then under the rule of the Jesuit Order, and the good Père in his account tells amusingly of the suspicious way in which the authorities regarded the visitors. They evidently thought the French might mean to take possession of some part of the country. All the French officers and indeed the Father himself had their movements closely watched. But every facility was given for repairs and to supply the vessels. The Government would willingly receive the Acadians as subjects, and private offers were made to them to remain. Offers were made to some of the officers also to enter the service of the country. But De Bougainville cut matters short by ordering a speedy departure, though the Acadians, tired of the sea, would gladly have remained. At length they reached the Malouine Islands situated some four hundred miles east of Cape Horn. They found the Islands a treeless, grass-covered country, swept by the ceaseless winds of the South Atlantic with no inhabitants but the penguins, which lined the shores in thousands like sentinels, and the stupid sea lions, animals of the seal species, which lay on the rocks, and opened their large mouths in defiance and wonder at the intrusion of man. Some of the young Acadians amused themselves by throwing pebbles into the gaping mouths of these animals, which they swallowed without winking.

The Islands were without wood or any fuel, and building materials had to be brought from Patagonia, four hundred miles distant. The settlers were very much discouraged but the good Père headed a party who went exploring for deposits of turf, and found some which was used as fuel. They set to work to form a settlement and used the stone at hand for building houses. But theirs was to be the fate of those "Who build, who build, But who enter not in." For a few years later another war arose with England and a British force came and captured the Malouines, whose name was changed to Falklands, and they have since remained a British colony.

The Acadians again departed, some going to the mainland of South America, where their identity as a separate people ceased.

Those who remained in Isle St. Jean and cast in their lot with us did better, we are now a united and assimilated people; they share in all our privileges, and produce their full quota of our clergymen, teachers, legislators, doctors and lawyers. For them has indeed been realized the prophecy or legend current among the early settlers that the new occupant of Stukeley farm, St. Peter's, was visited by the spirit of the former Acadian owner who said:

"Peace unto thee, Anglais, for not until a white house crowns each hill, and a mill stands by each stream shall the French possess the land again."

However improbably the fulfillment of this may seem; farmers should not be too ready to consult the C.F.F.C. for their fate.

J. Bambrick, Glen Roy
P.E.I. Magazine
February 1902

1760

After several shipwrecked survivors came ashore and settled the area, the name Naufrage (the French word for shipwreck) was chosen for the community.

1770

ANNABELLA — RELUCTANT NEWCOMERS

Sixty Scottish families boarded the *Annabella* in 1770, bound for the Carolinas. Imagine the dismay of these immigrants when they came within sight of St. John's Island where nothing but spruce and pine trees could be seen, right down to water's edge. They had been expecting the lush cultivated farms surrounding Princetown, their anticipated destination.

Shock was to be compounded when the *Annabella* ran onto a sandbar as they neared the shore. No lives were lost but all aboard had to be taken by lifeboats to land. Before night fell, some clothing and food was removed from the ship, but most was left for the next day.

That night however, a storm came up, the ship broke to pieces and all supplies were lost. This event occurred in Lot 18 (Malpeque) and Acadians there helped the shipwrecked settlers make shelters among the trees. The people lived there all winter, surviving on dried corn, oysters dug from under the shore ice and sea-cow flippers.

In the spring, with on-going help from the Acadians, they built homes, put in crops and were soon joined by 70 more Scottish settlers.

The spirit of the *Annabella* lives on at Cabot Reach Park where Scottish Heritage Days are held from time to time to commemorate the arrival of the brigantine from Campbelltown, Scotland, in October 1770.

SEA COWS — EXTERMINATED

The first law passed by the governor-in-council of the early 1770s, the regime of Governor Patterson, was an act regulating the fishery of sea cows, which were being rapidly exterminated by some fishermen from the Magdalene Islands and New England. From the time of Cartier, large numbers of sea cows were slain in their feeding grounds on our north shore and about the Magdalenes. For many centuries their precious oil and tough hides had meant death for thousands upon thousands of those strange beasts. On shore even the greatest, in spite of his powerful bulk of two tons, fell helpless to the harpoons of the hunters.

Patterson permitted only licensed hunting of sea cows in order to save them. They were, however, gradually killed off and Prince Edward Island lost a valuable source of industry.

The only reminder today of these great mammals is a community "up west" called Sea Cow Pond — reportedly named for the number of skeletons of sea cows found in the vicinity.

1775

THOMAS CURTIS' SWEETEST MORSEL

A young man by the name of Thomas Curtis has gone down in history as an important source of information about the early years of European settlement on Prince Edward Island. In 1775 Thomas boarded the brigantine, *Elizabeth*, in England. A trained timberman, he had been told that sawyers were better paid, and that land was available for fourpence per acre on a lease for life, or a free title for one shilling per acre. It seemed a dream come true for Thomas and he set sail with other passengers anticipating a great future in a new land.

Thomas kept a journal of his travels, which today is much valued for the insight it provides into daily life. His words were factual, one presumes; certainly not a gloried accounting of Island life. One event which he recorded was the wreck of the *Elizabeth.*

After a long voyage the *Elizabeth* arrived offshore of New London in November. It was evening, and although those on the boat could see the lights from the houses ashore the Captain decided it would be safer to wait for daylight before entering the harbour.

Unfortunately as dawn came, so did a change in the wind. The *Elizabeth* was driven off-shore in a gale which blew fiercely for three days. On November 5th, just before midnight, a lookout spotted land "on the lee bow," but shallow water and several sandbars lay between the ship and shore.

The winds changed again, this time driving the *Elizabeth* towards shore. All anchors but one failed to hold, and the masts were gone. The crew and passengers were in a very dangerous situation. Should the winds change again they could be driven off-shore again, this time in very poor condition to withstand the elements. The captain and first mate decided to cut the cable of the one remaining anchor in hopes that waves would lift the ship over the sandbars at high tide, and beach her.

The plan met with some success. The *Elizabeth* was driven over four sandbars, but stuck on the fifth and there she stayed, wrecked at the narrows off Lot 11, probably east of Cavendish inlet. The crew and passengers were able to reach the shore using the ship's lifeboats. Women and children had to sit in the bottom of the boats, up to their waists in water, to prevent themselves from being tossed out by the waves.

One of the passengers, a Mr. Fry, had tinder and flint for making a fire and, once on shore, he kindled a fire to dry their clothes. They had no axes, so had to use pocket knives to cut branches from fir trees to keep the fire burning and to build a wigwam. They had no food, so Mr. Fry and two of the sailors set off in a small boat to look for a settlement.

The wind dropped on the third day, calming the sea, and allowing half a dozen men to board the *Elizabeth* in search of food. They found a half a puncheon of rum, some sides of bacon, feather beds, blankets and cordage. A cask of oatmeal was washed ashore, but the end had been knocked out by the waves, letting the sand into the cask.

Starving people scooped away the sand, then stuffed the raw oatmeal into their mouths. Initial hunger appeased, the women made the remaining oatmeal into cakes and roasted them in the fire. One woman gave Thomas Curtis a piece of one of the cakes and a bit of pickled herring. Later he wrote in his journal, "This I thought was the sweetest morsel I ever ate in my life, though the outside was burnt black, the middle not half done."

Nine days after the wreck, a boat with supplies arrived from Malpeque (30 miles distant). Curtis recorded his share of the food as an eel and two potatoes. The women and children were taken by boat to New London about 46 miles away.

The next day three whaleboats arrived from New London with food, tools, and men to assist in salvaging what they could from the wreck. It must be remembered that everything these people had was aboard the *Elizabeth*, as well as supplies for the small settlement. The weather turned so cold, however, that it was decided to leave three men to guard the things saved while the other twenty-one men made their way to Malpeque.

The following winter was very hard on the newcomers. Food was in short supply because the supplies for the local agent had been lost. He did let each family have a barrel of flour; which was used to supplement salt fish and potatoes. The settlement consisted of some sixteen log cabins in a clearing in the woods. Curtis soon had enough of New London and began to pine for the old London he had left behind.

He left in May on the first ship after a final meal of fresh flat fish and white bread,which he recorded as "such as I never tasted before on the Island."

ELIZABETH — ADVENTURE FROM A WOMAN'S EYE

Although it may seem we are devoting too much of our space to the *Elizabeth*, the fact that we have this sinking from the perspective of a woman cannot be overlooked. It is too easy to forget how many women came to settle the Island, often in very perilous conditions. As well, Thomas Curtis in the preceding accounting and Penlope Stewart were of different social status — and thus had a slightly different experience. The following accounting was obtained from the Public Archives of Prince Edward Island (#2308) where it had been transcribed from handwritten notes.

In 1775 Chief Justice Peter Stewart and family, en route here from Scotland, were wrecked off Cascumpec. The following account of their experience was given to Hon. Benj. Davies by a daughter of the Chief Justice, Miss Penlope Stewart, who subsequently married Mr. Jas. MacNutt of Malpeque.

My father chartered a brig to bring us over; she was an English vessel with an English crew and on board, besides our family and servants, several of my father's people, who intended settling on land in the colony, for he had two townships granted him by the King, George III. We had made ample provision for ourselves, as far as food was concerned and added an additional supply of pork and oatmeal sufficient to last two years. We embarked at Greenock and sailed down the beautiful Clyde to the ocean. Although I was only ten years old, I felt very lonely on leaving our dear old Scotland, the well beloved home that I shall never forget.

We left Scotland during the last week in July 1775. The weather during our voyage was very capricious; sometimes it was fine, sometimes terrific storms would beat over and around us, storms that made the timbers creak and the vessel lurch, besides filling us with such a sense of loneliness and homesickness and heart sickness as well. At last, sometime in the latter part of

October, we made Cape Breton; then several days later we reached Prince Edward Island. We learned after that the Captain had made a mistake — thought he was on the south side of the Island and it was the North.

During the night a heavy gale sprang up, so heavy that it drove the ship ashore and we had small hope of saving ourselves, but providence was kind; by morning the wind abated and the morning showed us a dreary shore with nothing but breakers raging along the beach. The sea subsided however, and all the seamen launched the small boat, found a landing place where all were landed, with a stock of provisions, clothing, etc. The men made a great fire and we passed the night in the woods, with, it is needless to say, the most gloomy apprehensions.

When morning broke, the wind rose to a perfect hurricane accompanied with snow, and then we learned that the ship had broken to pieces, Not a vestige remained. What made our position more desolate was the fact that the ground was covered with snow and the provisions we had would only last a week.

We all thought that the breaking up of the ship was the final touch to our misfortunes, but it turned out to be the saving of us all, for as the wind blew in its fury it drifted upon the shore pieces of the wreck, with parts of the rigging and sails together with casks of beef, pork, oatmeal and flour. How we thanked God for our deliverance, and how cheerfully the men secured the material, that had practically speaking, saved our lives!

The next day they went to work and built two camps, two large ones, one for our family and attendants, and the other for the ship's company and emigrants [sic]. Both camps were covered with the ship's sails which effectively protected us from the wind, rain and snow, and the hordfrost [sic] of the long winters. Here we remained for months, learning absolutely nothing of our position although my brothers, at different times penetrated into the forest in the expectation of discovering an inhabitant; but the frost was so severe and the snow so deep that they could only travel a short distance from camp.

About mid-winter we were surprised by a visit of an Indian hunter, who with snowshoes could travel forty miles a day, could speak English and was an intelligent fellow. My father had a long conversation with him, during which he learned that we were at Cascumpec, on the North side of the Island, forty miles in a direct line from Malpeque [afterwards the home of the MacNeils] and about one hundred miles from Charlottetown.

The Indian said in the Spring of the year, when the ice cleared away, he would come and take my father, in his canoe, to Malpeque, where he thought he could find a guide to conduct him to Charlottetown; if he failed he would guide him himself through the woods. So my father engaged our Indian for the purpose of taking him to Charlottetown.

Then five months were spent in that dreary solitude before the cry of the wild geese announced the advent of Spring. A couple of weeks after the first cry of the wild goose, true to his promise, the Indian made his appearance with his canoe, which had been laid up about a mile from our camp. Then my father proceeded with him, through the narrow passage of water, protected from the sea by a range of sand banks leading from Cascumpec to Malpeque harbour.

It was then well on towards the latter part of June, and one day one of our people brought the joyful news that a schooner was in the offing, standing in the harbour; it proved to be a vessel my father had sent from Charlottetown for us. My brothers got us safely around the coast and on board the schooner, after which we immediately set sail, and in a couple of days we were in Charlottetown, and in civilized society once more; it being our eleven months since we left the dear old Scottish Shores behind us.

1775

PIRATES OR PRIVATEERS?

In 1775, North America once more resounded with the din of war and on one occasion even the little Island of Saint John (as we were then known) was jarred from its usual serenity. It all began and ended with pirates or privateers — which, you can judge for yourself — invading the peaceful capital.

In October, 1775, General George Washington, commander of the rebel army, learned that two English brigs were on their way to Quebec with arms and stores. He sent two armed schooners, the ***Lynch*** *of six guns and manned by seventy men and the* ***Franklin*** *of four guns and sixty men, to the Saint Lawrence to intercept the*

> *supply ships. The two captains, Broughton and Selman, were to receive in payment for their privateering one-third of the value of all prizes, but they warned not to molest any Canadian ships which were not taking part in the war.*

The unscrupulous duo ignored their orders and on November 17th the *Lynch* and the *Franklin* appeared in Charlottetown Harbour. Little thinking that they were in danger, the inhabitants went quietly on with their work.

> *The Americans showed their true intentions by landing two parties, the glint of whose arms could be seen from the shore. Phillips Callbeck, acting-governor in Patterson's absence, thinking that they would be less likely to burn the town if they met with no resistance, went alone to the landing place to face them. But his civility was met with brusqueness and boorishness. He was ordered aboard one of the ships and was not allowed to return home. As he boarded the vessel he was struck across the mouth. Soon after a messenger came to Callbeck and demanded the keys of the house and stores or they would batter down the doors. The privateers broke into three stores and carried off to their vessels the people's winter provisions.*

The Callbeck home was the next scene of outrage. These men, who should have been on the Saint Lawrence had they obeyed orders, were not content until they had carried off every article of value in the house. They stripped the floors, undraped the windows, dismantled the beds, looted the clothes closets, rifled the chests, plundered the larder, and committed a host of depredations too numerous to mention. Everything was taken to the ships — not even a candle was left in the pantry. They made merry in the wine cellar, drinking one cask of wine to the dregs, while others made off somewhat unsteadily towards the ship with the rest of the liquors.

In Mrs. Callbeck's bedroom they pried open drawers and trunks, scattering her clothes about the room, and they read her letters. Finding her not at home the marauders searched the town that they might cut her throat because her father, a Mr. Coffin of Boston, had remained loyal to the British cause. Fortunately she escaped, some say by running down a stream and hiding, others say because she was at her husband's farm, some four miles away.

Broughton, Selman and crew then ransacked the acting-governor's office taking among other things, the Province's silver seal and Governor Patterson's commission. They then ransacked and sacked the governor's house and climaxed their eventful visit by carrying off the Church furniture which had been stored there for safekeeping. On their way to the wharf, they made Mr. Wright a surveyor-general, a prisoner and laughed at the tears of his wife and sister, mocking them with insulting words.

Soon aboard the two schooners all was in readiness for departure. Callbeck remonstrated with the two captains, pointing out that they would be dismissed in all probability for disobeying orders. He entreated them to make restitution for their own sake and for the sake of the eighty new settlers who would be left to perish in want without means or sustenance. But his plea fell on deaf ears. The two ships sailed and the townsfolk heaved a sigh of relief; but the three captured Islanders wondered if ever again they would see those homes so fast disappearing on the horizon.

At Canso the privateers seized a ship on its way to the Island with a councillor and his wife and a chaplain, the Reverend Theophilus Des Brisay. These passengers were taken by the privateers but were soon released. Fourteen days later, the New Englanders reached Winter Harbour 110 miles east of Cambridge where was Washington's headquarters. George Washington freed the prisoners with profound apologies. Captains Broughton and Selman he dismissed from their commands. But the stolen articles were not restored. Callbeck, who had lost 2,000 pounds' worth of property, complained afterwards that he saw his wife's rings and bracelets adorning the "female connections of these villains." The Islanders lost no time getting out of the country as they were afraid that Washington might change his mind.

THE ISLAND GETS A MAN-OF-WAR

When Callbeck reached home he petitioned the Home Government to send a man-of-war for protection of the Island. During the summer of 1776, His Majesty's armed brig, the *Diligent,* was stationed at Charlottetown. In the fall it was relieved by the *Hunter,* sloop of war, which brought arms and ammunition from Halifax. Later four companies of soldiers were sent from New York and barracks were built. But the Island was not seriously disturbed again. Privateers occasionally raided along the eastern shore, stealing primarily sheep. And of course Georgetown was raided. At Charlottetown, British frigates were a common sight and people gathered more than once on the wharf to see some captured ship towed into the harbour — a stirring spectacle indeed! The prisoners were usually escorted by our garrisons to Halifax.

In 1778, a second expedition was launched against the Island but met with no success. Two whale boats fitted out in Machias, a small town in Maine, reached Pictou. Here the reels seized a valuable armed merchant ship taking on cargo for Scotland and brought it to Baie Verte to await reinforcements. They planned to raid Charlottetown and carry off the cannon at Fort Amherst. But they never reached their destination. The commander of the **Hunter** *sent a sloop after the captured ship. When the sloop arrived at Baie Verte it was found that the rebels had turned the ship over to its mate and had scudded for shore. She was taken to Charlottetown and given up to her commander. Thus, as far as our story is concerned, ended the Revolutionary War and piratical raids.*

The Story of Old Abegweit
George Edward Hart
1935

November 19th, 1791 — During the violent snow storm on the 4th instant, a brig belonging to Antigua, called the **Eliza**, *James Craig, master, bound from Quebec to the West Indies, was wrecked at Cape Torment, near the Pond on the north side of the island. Her cargo, which consisted principally of provisions and lumber, was saved but the vessel is entirely lost.*

Saturday, December 17, 1791 — The schooner **Endeavour**, *W.A. Perry, master, cleared outwards at the custom house on Monday last for Antigua, with a cargo of fish and lumber. In this vessel Captain Craig, of the brig* **Eliza** *which was unfortunately cast away at Cape Torment some time since, and a gentleman by the name of Burke, passenger, together with the crew of the said brig, will take their departure for the same place.*

Royal Gazette and Miscellany of the Island of St. John
Number XI, Volume I
published every fortnight

1791 H.M. *Alert,* schooner, went down in Charlottetown Harbour

1792 *Betsey,* a schooner wrecked off East Point. The brigantine *Abegail,* went down off Cape Tryon.

Monday, May 2, 1792 — The schooner ***Abigail, Elliot,*** *with passengers from the American states, was unfortunately drove on the bar in coming into New London Harbour during the high wind of Tuesday last, and in the course of the night went to pieces, previous to which the passengers and crew had been all safely landed.*
Royal Gazette and Miscellaney of the Island of St. John
Number XXII, Volume I

AN ERA OF SHIPBUILDING

Few ships of large tonnage were built in this province although a considerable number were constructed for the British coasting trade. From the Richards shipyard in Bideford came the *Flora,* which was perhaps the largest but two of Island vessels. The yard launched almost a hundred ships, valued at over a million and a half dollars, in the forty years it was in operation. Charlottetown, too, had her share. At least five shipyards hummed with industry along the waterfront from Kensington Rifle Range to Dundas Esplanade. From the Duncan yards came two famous ships. The ship *Gertrude* constructed of birch, pine, oak and hackmatack, was a Liverpool transport during the Indian Mutiny and later an Australian emigrant ship. At the Duncan shipyard, the largest vessel ever built on the Island was christened the *Ethel.* The launching of the *Ethel,* a full-model three-deck ship of 1795 tons, was a great event and people came from far and near to see her slide down the ways.

"She starts, — she moves, — she seems to feel
The thrill of life along her keel,
And, spurning with her foot the ground,
With one exulting, joyous bound,
She leaps into the ocean's arms."

At first, Island men were only builders and financiers who built their ships to sell abroad, not to sail themselves. Most of the smaller vessels were used in the coasting trade and the larger ones were loaded with timber and sold, cargo and all, in England and occasionally in the West Indies. But Islanders came to realize that they had other products to sell to the outside world. There were the products which they won from the soil with their scythe, sickle, cradle and hoe — the potatoes, oats, barley and wheat. There were the cattle fattened on rich green Island pastures. And the women's work at the spinning-wheel and loom was no less excellent. Their homespun cloth was used by farmers, sailors and lumbermen, and was even demanded in the aristocratic homes of the Old Country. The farmers' sons took to the sea in Island ships and carried goods to Halifax, Cape Breton, Newfoundland, the West Indies, Great Britain and even farther afield. They crossed the equator where "Old Neptune" proclaimed them salts; they weathered Cape Horn, the Cape of Storms; and they sailed the seven seas. "Out of a class of boys from one county district school, thirteen schoolmates became shipmasters." Island seamen became noted for their great skill and physique. Point Prim gave perhaps more men to the sea than any other district. These were the descendants of the Skye Pioneers, hardy men, rugged men, men born to command, kings of the sea. But all was not glory in that tale of the sea. Many a mother or wife mourned the loss of a beloved one, for the sea had taken its toll. But more and more did Islanders seek the treasure of the world in their swift sailing ships. When the wind was favourable an old salt would say that the sovereigns could be heard rolling down the topsail sheets, so good was foreign trade.

Island vessels found many uses. The larger ships were known on the high seas and in the emigrant and transport business. The smaller ones were used in the coasting trade and in the Bank and ice-seal fisheries.

The Story of Old Abegweit
George Edward Hart, Teacher of History,
Prince Street School,
Charlottetown, P.E.I. 1935

ADVENTURE

Disasters didn't happen only to large ships. Sometimes it was a fisherman who found himself in trouble. One such man was Captain James Richard, who decided to take his sister Abigail and cousin Sophie on board the schooner *Adventure* for a fishing voyage. Such an event was not common practice, but occasionally a skipper would enjoy having his family with him.

An unexpected snow storm drove the schooner ashore at Souris.

The captain fastened one girl to the rail and the other to the windlass to keep them from being washed overboard by the crashing waves. The cook tried to look after Sophie, while the captain gave his overcoat, oil-skins, and rubber hat to protect her from the cold. Just before daybreak Sophie died from the cold and exposure. The mate also died. Abigail and the rest of the fishermen were rescued by men who rowed out from Souris and lowered them by ropes into a dory.

DISASTROUS FIRST VOYAGE FOR BRIG *JABEZ*

Imagine the overwhelming despair that must have been felt by those who laboured to build the brig *Jabez* when they learned that she went down on her maiden voyage.

> *The new brig,* ***Jabez*** *,Grigg Master from Richmond Bay, P.E. Island bound for Bideford, on her first voyage was wrecked on Cape St. Lawrence, on the western coast of Cape Breton, at 8 a.m. on the 6th of November, and soon after went to pieces. The crew with much difficulty, got to land, with the exception of two, John Hay, brother-in-law to Capt. Grigg, and Richard Westlake, an apprentice, who were dashed to pieces among the rocks.*
>
> *The survivors, many of them almost in a state of nudity, after travelling about six miles through thick woods, came upon a small settlement of Scotch emigrants, consisting of three families only, who lived thirty miles apart from any other settlement.*
>
> *Here the shipwrecked mariners remained for about ten days, until they were sufficiently recovered to proceed to the nearest port. Capt. Grigg, who together with his sons and two of the seamen had since arrived in Charlottetown, speaks in the warmest terms of the kindness they received from those poor people, who, during their stay, slaughtered two of their cattle for their support without the slightest prospect of renumeration. Their names which are well worthy of honourable mention, are MacLean, Macintosh, and Higley.*
>
> P.E.I. newspaper clipping
> collection (undated)

1803

THE SKYE PIONEERS

Islanders of Scottish descent hold a monument near Eldon in high esteem. It honours the *Polly*, a ship some say is cherished and remembered with the same affection as the *Mayflower* in New England. It was the good ship *Polly* that bore the Skye Pioneers to our shores. These Highland Scots were fleeing a land where they had been driven from their lands and were living in poverty when the Earl of Selkirk asked them to cross the Atlantic and pioneer a land described as fertile, with food to spare and land for all. They agreed and boarded ships bound for Prince Edward Island.

The *Polly* arrived first, after an eventful voyage. According to tradition she narrowly escaped pirates, became jammed in an Arctic ice flow and was hailed by a man-o'-war in search of able bodied seamen. Legend has it that the captain of the *Polly* escaped Jack Tar by replying that his passengers and crew were down with the much-dreaded ship-fever. On August 7th, 1803, she came to anchor in Orwell Bay and was soon followed by the *Dykes* and the *Oughten*. Altogether the three ships, brought out eight hundred hardy Scots of all ages and embracing every trade.

1813

YANKEE FREEBOOTER

In 1813, during the American War, Messrs. Mcougan, McKendrick, Mathews and Woodside, of Malpeque, built a vessel, of 50 tons burthen for the Newfoundland trade, loaded her with cattle and all sailed in her with Matthew Stewart as Captain. Off Cape Ray they were met by an American Privateer and were taken. A Yankee crew were put on board of her under the same captain, and the other Islanders were taken away in the privateer. The Yankees intended to take the Malpeque vessel as a prize to the United States.

They had not sailed far before an English cutter came up with them, when the Americans hoisted British colors to deceive; but Captain Stewart, as the English men drew near, jumped up and down, waved his hat in the air and by other demonstrations, show that all was not right. The British boarded the yankee prize, retook her, and taking the Yankees prisoners, put two negroes on board the Malpeque craft with Capt. Stewart, to return to the Island whilst the cutter set off in search of the privateer.

Captain Stewart, being afraid of the blacks could not sleep nor rest. The vessel at last ran ashore on the Magdalen Islands, and her crew of three were saved all right; but three young widows were left in Malpeque to mourn the loss of their husbands who were lost in the Yankee freebooter.

The Presbyterian
November 22, 1877

1823

JESSIE

LAUNCHED: On Tuesday last a fine brig was launched from the yard of Messrs. D. MacKay & Co. A great concourse of ladies and gentlemen were present, and we are happy to say, she slided into her destined element to the delight of spectators, and the satisfaction of those enterprising gentlemen and their builders.

The Prince Edward Island Register
November 8, 1823

One long ago Christmas Day, in 1823, a ship called the *Jessie* set sail from Prince Edward Island, the ultimate fate of which became a matter of great importance and concern to the inhabitants of Charlottetown. The melancholy circumstance is recalled by a clipping from the *Prince Edward Island Register.* The clipping, prefaced by an extract from McGregors *History of Prince Edward Island,* was printed in the *Prince Edward Island Magazine* in 1903.

There is scarcely a more melancholy catastrophe than that of the ship ***Jessie*** *which occurred in 1823. The vessel with Mr. Donald McKay, the owner and some other passengers, and the master and crew, seventy-six in number, left the harbor of Three Rivers (Georgetown), in Prince Edward Island; and as the ship was observed off the coast of Cape Breton, near Cheticamp, during a snowstorm on the 27th of December, it is probable she struck in* *the night on St. Paul's Island. In the month of May following (no account having before been received of the vessel) it was reported that some fishermen had discovered the wreck of a ship, and a number of bodies on St. Paul's Island. On this report a schooner was dispatched thence from Charlottetown, the people on board of which found the wreck of the* **Jessie** *and the bodies of eleven men, who must have perished by the intense cold soon after landing; the remainder of the crew, it is likely, were either washed overboard by the surf, or lost in attempting to get up the cliff. The bodies of McKay and the master were carried to Charlottetown; nothing could be more melancholy than their funerals, which were attended by the greatest concourse of people ever known in Charlottetown to accompany the remains of any person to the mansions of the dead. I had for some years enjoyed the friendship of this gentleman. I was one of the last that parted with him on leaving the Island; and six months afterward I saw his body laid in the grave. When I say that few men have left the world more regretted by his acquaintance, that in his manners he was truly a gentleman; and that he possessed in an imminent degree all the kind and good qualities which gain the hearts and esteem of men, no one who knew him will say that I exaggerate. He was born to Scotland, served His Majesty for some years, and was taken on the coast of France and remained ten years a prisoner in that country. — McGregor*

On Tuesday last, the Schooner **Feronia** *arrived here from St. Paul's Island having on board the remains of Donald McKay, Esq., and Capt. McAlpin. The party sent on the melancholy expedition report that having reached the place of their destination, they disembarked at day-break and found within half a mile of the shore, eleven bodies, those of Messrs McKay and McAlpin included. Fifteen were yet wanting to complete the dismal list of sufferers, and for several hours they carefully explored the desolate rock in hopes of their meeting with them. Their search, however, was fruitless, not a trace of them being discoverable. After wrapping up the bodies of Mr. Mckay and Mr. McAlpin in tarred sheets, they deposited them in coffins, well prepared for the purpose, and then proceeded to perform the last melancholy office over the remaining nine, covering them with earth and sods, which they procured with great difficulty at a considerable distance. In the absence of information a great latitude is given to conjecture,* *and a variety of opinion have been broached, as to the possible length of time that elapsed from the landing of the unfortunate people upon the Island, and the period of their death. It appears however reasonable to suppose that their miseries were but of comparatively short duration, the cold having been very severe, and nothing found that could in any way have secured them from its effects. The* **Feronia** *called in at Margaree, where a writing desk, the property of Mr. McKay was found, and which was carried away by the persons who first discovered the wreck, it had been forced open; there was a great number of private letters and bills to a large amount forwarded in the* **Jessie**. *The wreck lies close to the cliff and is firmly wedged between two rocks. The sternpost and after part are entirely gone, but the bows and waist remain, and it is said that she has in her at lest 250 tons of timber. On the* **Feronia's** *entrance into the harbour, the strongest sensation was excited, and crowds of people assembled on shore; a high breeze and flowing tide brought the vessel slowly up the river, her colours half mast high. She anchored opposite the residence of D. MacKay, Esq., cousin to the deceased and in the course of the evening the bodies were brought on shore. During the interval between the arrival of the corpses and the period of their internment, the whole town wore an unusual gloom. The vessels in the harbour hoisted their flags half mast high, and the countenances of even strangers were saddened by the mournful scene. On Thursday the funeral took place, attended by an unusual train of friends from town and country.*

The bodies were carried into the church, where an appropriate anthem was sung by the choir, and the desk service read by the Rev. Mr. Aden. the procession then moved slowly on to the burial ground, and the Rev. Mr. Jenkins performed the remainder of the service.

The Prince Edward Island Register,
June 26, 1824

1826 The bark, HMS *Rifleman,* was lost south west of Wood Islands.

Winter mail services on Prince Edward Island as depicted by *Harper's Weekly*, April 6th, 1867. (Public Archives of Prince Edward Island 4045/1)

Ice crossings are somewhat re-enacted in ice-boat races held across the harbour, during the Charlottetown Winter Carnival. (*The Guardian*)

1827

CAPE TRAVERSE — PUSH OFF POINT FOR WINTER MAILS

The chief difficulty for the people of Prince Edward Island in this era had always been the passenger and mail communication with the outer world during the winter months. In the earliest times of the British occupation, crossings with boats were made from Wood Island at the south-eastern corner of Queen's county to Pictou Island and then to the town of Pictou, a distance of at least 23 miles, but so long and hazardous was the route that sometimes a number of weeks would pass without any passage being made.

Anyone who has experienced an Island winter storm will shudder at even the thought of being out on the open ice of Northumberland when the howling winds and sleeting snow hit. It must have been a horrific experience. I can remember driving in a heated car from Charlottetown to our country home in a blizzard that came up without warning. The car couldn't buck the high drifts so we had to abandon it and walk perhaps a quarter mile to the house. It was only through my husband's strength and will, and the luck of finding a fence to follow that we struggled into our house.

> *In 1827 the people of Cape Traverse conceived the idea of crossing to Cape Tormentine, a distance of only eight and a half or nine miles, Neil Campbell and Donald McInnis being the first to cross over. In this year some crossings were made and so confident was everybody of its great superiority over the Pictou route that some of the mails were sent during the following winter by this route. In 1829 an agreement was entered into between the government of the Island and the parties of Cape Traverse to carry the mails exclusively by this way. The boats named "ice-boats" used for the purpose are small, constructed as light as possible consistent with strength, and have runners on each side so they can be dragged over the snow and ice when necessary. Straps are attached to the sides and the boatmen and others have the other end fastened round their bodies either to assist in hauling the boat or to enable them to get on the ice again should their feet drop through.*
>
> *Passengers have to pay $2.00 for the privilege of going with the crew and still have to assist in getting the boat along, but by*

paying a double fare they can stay on board during the whole crossing. When there is a strip of water everyone gets in the boat and it is rowed, and when they came to a field of ice it is hauled up and dragged along. "Lolly" — that is, a considerable body of snow in the water not frozen, or fine ground up ice — is what is by far the most dreaded, as in it neither can the boat be rowed nor can men walk. As would be expected, a number of accidents have happened through unexpected snow storms having arisen after the departure of the boats, for there is now always a fleet of three going together. One happened in 1831, when three men and a passenger were overtaken. After being out all night and suffering terribly they were rescued next day by some people from Cape Egmont. In 1843, ten persons were out part of two days and a night — thirty-six hours in all. They also suffered severely, some being badly frozen, but about two o'clock in the afternoon of the second day they succeeded in reaching the Island shore.

A third accident took place in 1855, the worst of them all, for in it a Mr. Haszard of Charlottetown lost his life. He and another student returning from Philadelphia reached Cape Tormentine on Friday, March 9th, and in the morning these two with a third passenger, an elderly man named Wier, left with one boat's crew of four men for Cape Traverse. During the afternoon they had reached within half a mile of the Island side (of Northumberland Strait) when a blinding snow storm set in. They pushed on but were at last stopped by lolly. In these circumstances it was useless to make further attempt to reach the shore. Therefore the boat was drawn back on the ice and turned up to afford shelter for the party. With a bitter frost made far worse by a gale of wind, they were in a sad plight. For two days and three nights they suffered untold hardship and misery, from hunger, cold and exposure. On toward the third day they killed a dog belonging to Mr. Wier and this revived them so that they put on increased effort and, throwing over the trunks and baggage, they toiled on, having now drifted to within four or five miles from the Nova Scotia coast. By this time Mr. Haszard was unable to walk and on Monday evening he died. The others trudged on, and on Tuesday morning reached the shore near Wallace, but some two miles from the nearest house. Some reached there and gave the alarm and soon as were housed but very much frost-bitten. Mr. Wier lost all his fingers and his two feet, but he did not long survive his loss.

The last accident happened in 1885. At about 9:30 on the morning of January 27th, the day being a piercingly cold one, and after considerable consultation among the captains of the boats as to the advisability of attempting to cross, three boats set out from the Island side. The crews consisted of fifteen men together with seven passengers. During the forenoon a storm began which by noon had increased with the wind to a blinding drift. As evening approached they were met by a great deal of lolly and nothing remained but to stay on the ice all night. Two of the boats were turned up gunwale to gunwale at the top, so as to form a kind of house, and from the third boat they tore the tin with which each was covered, so as to make a sort of pan in which they could kindle a fire. First the newspapers were taken from the mail bags and set on fire and, later on, the third boat was broken up and all the extra oars so that some little warmth could be had; but this was a laborious undertaking, for there was no axe or other tool by which the breaking could be done. But while some warmth was obtained the smoke in their eyes added to their miseries, more perhaps than the fire lessened them. To make them still more wretched the fire was sufficient to melt the snow near and their clothing thus became soaked with water. Owing to the hardships he endured, one of the crew became delirious. As morning dragged slowly along there was no improvement in the weather and their fuel was nearly all burned. But about three o'clock in the afternoon, the storm moderated somewhat and the Island shores could be faintly made out some distance to the north. After great exertion the board ice, that is, the smooth flat ice from the shore, in distinction from the hillocky ice floating up and down the straits was reached. But still their troubles were not over. They were met on the land by great drifts of snow almost impossible to wade through, especially as their clothes were now frozen stiff upon their limbs. By making shouts and screams they were at last heard, and a search party, after great exertion and considerable hunting, succeeded in getting the whole twenty-two into comfortable quarters. One man, a Mr Fraser, lost almost all his fingers and toes, so badly were his limbs frozen. The boatman who had become delirious did not long suvive the fearful privations they all endured. This party was thirty-six hours in the straits.

Past and Present of Prince Edward Island

From then until the advent of icebreakers to the Island, the federal government managed the ice-boat service. Crossings were only undertaken when the ice at the eastern end of the Island was too thick and too much packed by the easterly winds of March to enable the winter steamers to reach Pictou.

1830 – 1831

SMOKE – BOATS

The ***Richard Smith*** *was the first vessel to enter Charlottetown harbour without the usual show of sail. People stood and gazed as we might today if we saw a rocket ship. The Indians of Point Prim regarded the "smoke-boats" with superstitious awe and the citizens thronged the wharf in wonderment. Little did they realize that soon a sooty cloud issuing from ten thousand funnels would stifle their graceful ocean birds which, with snowy wings and body poised, skimmed the seven seas. The days of sail would pass and that ship, the* ***Richard Smith*** *of Pictou, marked the beginning of the end. Before leaving the steamer took Governor Ready and his friends for a short cruise up the Hillsborough River. In September of the next year [1831] the* ***Royal William*** *called here on her way from Halifax to Quebec. This Canadian ship was the first vessel to cross the Atlantic entirely under steam.*

The Story of Old Abegweit
George Edward Hart
1935

1835

CADMUS — HARROWING EXPERIENCE OF LITTLE MARY PARRY

Mr. Parry, of this town, and his daughter, eight years of age, sailed from Charlottetown, in the ***Cadmus****, on the 27th November. After beating about the Gulf three nights, during very severe cold and heavy gales, the topsail and foresail carried away, with the* *standing jib and main boom; the foresail frozen to the deck, the running rigging fast in the blocks, and the vessel consequently quite unmanageable, she drifted, on the fourth day, on Cape Breton, at Broad Cove.*

Providentially the schooner, which was strongly built and well fastened, held together, and was driven by a heavy surf so near the shore, that, on the receding of the tide, four of the hands succeeded, by the assistance of the hospitable people on the beach, who threw a lead and line on board, in getting on 'terra firma', but Mr. Parry had the anxious part of watching his child during a most inclement night, himself almost in a perishing state, and the vessel one sheet of ice — the spray finding its way into the berth where the little girl lay, covered or secured by wet clothes; yet, in this lamentable situation, not a murmuring word escaped her; her language was calculated to inspire confidence in others!

Next day, about 10 o'clock, one of the settlers succeeded in getting on board, and contrived to rig a basket, in which the child was taken on shore, where she soon rallied, and made herself quite happy and at home with her new acquaintances, the children of their kind host, although a stranger to their language as well as to their persons. After a recruit of a fortnight, Mr. Parry and daughter, in company with a fellow-survivor (Mr. Louttit, the mate, who greatly assisted in taking care of the little girl), commenced Dec. 14, an arduous journey of more than 300 miles in one of the most inclement seasons on record.

It is easier to conceive than to portray the privations and sufferings a female child must endure on such a journey, amidst drifts, deep snows, intense frost, scanty and indifferent provision, and inconvenient lodging; yet little Mary manifest a spirit of heroism and cheerfulness rarely surpassed by a grown person of either sex; and, to crown all, in crossing the Northumberland Straits, she gallantly, where the ice was good, ran along, laying hold of the rope to assist in drawing the boat; and could find cause of amusement, when her companions occasionally broke through the ice. Probably Mary Parry, if not the only, is the youngest child who ever crossed the Strait on the ice.

The Royal Gazette
January 12, 1836

1836

NEPTUNE RETURNS TOMMY TUPLIN

Tommy Tuplin (1830-1920) spent many years of his life operating the Black Horse Inn. Thomas was the sixth child of Reuben and Rebecca Tuplin, who had come to Prince Edward Island from England, in a voyage that was the source of great drama. The story is told in the book *All Their Tuplin Children*, written by Lloyd James Miller.

A severe wind storm hit the ship carrying the Tuplin family as it neared Newfoundland in June 1836. Many of the passengers were seasick, including Rebecca, Tommy's mother. His father, Reuben, decided to take Rebecca up the ladder from the hold to the deck, and open the scuttle enough to allow her a breath of fresh air. Little Tommy, then aged 6, was a curious chap and not to be left behind. He crept behind his parents up the ladder.

Just as they arrived on deck, a huge wave came towards them and a mass of rolling foam washed over the side of the boat. The frantic parents watched helplessly as their Tommy rolled and tumbled in the water, snatched from them he was washed overboard. Even as the crew rushed to help, the boy was drifting from them. Rope and life preservers fell short of their mark and Tommy's cries were soon lost in the roar of the storm.

Even though Reuben and fellow sympathizers urged Rebbeca to go below, away from the scene of the tragedy, she refused. Clinging to the rail of the ship Rebecca called out to her son, who was by now just a speck in the turbulent seas.

"Please Lord, take me and spare our Tommy," she prayed aloud. Those witnessing the mother's grief silently echoed her prayer.

Suddenly the sea became very still; just for a moment. Then another giant wave formed, this time pulling the small boy along on its crest, as it raced towards the ship. His mother screamed for her boy to be returned. All stood immobilized as they watched him hurtle closer and closer. Then, as the wave hit, they grabbed for anything that would hold them secure as the water washed over the boat.

Tommy was thrown against the rat-lines on the mast of the boat. When his father reached for him, Tommy's fingers had to be pried one by one from the ropes, even though he was unconscious.

Even though his return was seen as a miracle, few had faith in the boy's recovery and advised his mother to let him die in peace. Rebecca refused to stand aside.

She called for a tub of warm water with a little turpentine added. Gently she lowered Tommy into the bath until his little body was warmed. Drying him off, he laid him onto the bed in the captain's cabin and sat by his side, keeping vigil. After a time, Tommy stirred and asked for a little sugar, a treat in those days that would equal candy today. He was given a little, enough to make him smile, and everyone present was assured that little Tommy Tuplin was on the mend.

He grew to be a successful innkeeper and family man. He married Anne Blaney and they operated Black Horse Inn together. It was a busy life, for the couple had 12 children, all born at the Inn.

Guardian columnist Frances Carruthers recorded this tale and noted that in 1869 the community met to vote on whether or not they would allow them to operate a tavern at the crossroads. This procedure was in accordance with the *Scott Act* which dealt with the sale of liquor and spirits. Permission was granted. In 1880 Thomas Tuplin gave up this business and moved to Indian River where he started a saw and grist mill.

Although the Inn has long since gone, there is a monument, topped with a black horse, at the crossroads of the Irishtown Road where it intersects the road from Indian River to Margate. The site is known as Black Horse Corner. This route marks one of the earliest roads on the Island, and probably the longest at the time. It was built around 1800 from Charlottetown to Princetown. Several people perished from cold and hunger on this lonely route,so the Inn and a stable were built by Gov. Edmund Fanning at his own expense. It eventually came into the hands of Thomas Tuplin.

It is interesting to note that a relative of Tuplin's, who had come to the Island some years earlier, settled eventually in Summerside. At one time during their stay in that community, the roads became so muddy that a cow drowned in the middle of Lower Spring Street.

1836

The *Esperance* was cast ashore on the north coast of Prince Edward Island near New London Bay in the autumn of 1836. Copies of extensive paperwork hardwritten from the Customs House in Halifax are on file at the Public Archives of Prince Edward Island. Her sails and running rigging were sold by the master. The hull of the vessel was thence sold off to a Mr. Peter Sutherland of Chaleur Bay who succeeded in getting the vessel off put her into repair and had fresh sails and running rigging put on her at a cost of £1,000. An unexpected difficulty occurred in getting the vessel registered *de novo* at Prince Edward Island and resulted in absolutely reams of paperwork in hard-to-decipher hand.

Even when the seas appear calm, waves dashing against the rocks can be treacherous as depicted in this photo found at a Prince Edward Island flea market. The man shown looks like he could well have been a survivor from a wreck; dressed in his skivies, he even has his shoes and socks on.

1837 - 1839

SHIPPING INTELLIGENCE

The following listings from the *Colonial Herald and the Prince Edward Island Advertiser* are typical examples of the dangers facing ships plying the coastal waters of Prince Edward in the mid-1800s. These records also track what happened to several vessels after the actual stranding, founding or other accident. They offer one explanation as to why a ship will appear to have been wrecked several times. Often a boat that ran aground would be sold, or auctioned off. The buyer would then repair and refit, and it would be put back in service. Another explanation is that, over the years, and from different countries names are sure to be duplicated.

Saturday, September 2, 1837 — The American fishing schooner ***Ariadne****, Sylus Howard, master, of Gloucester, Mass., put into Souris in a leaky state, a few days ago, and has been condemned and sold there, for the benefit of the underwriters. She had previously lost part of her keel, and sustained other damage, having been five hours on the western part of Malpec bar during a gale, on the 10th ultimo.*

Saturday, September 9, 1837 — The Brig ***Jane*** *of Waterford, Whalen, master, from Miramichi, bound to Cardiff, has been totally lost on Fish Island, at the entrance of Richmond Bay. Crew saved.*

Saturday, September 16, 1837 — An American schooner (name unknown) was lost off Caribou on the night of Wednesday, the 13th inst., with all the crew. She is supposed to have mistaken Caribou for the entrance of Pictou Harbour. The brig ***Highlander****, belonged to Mr. Hatton, of Pictou, is on shore at River John, without any prospect of being got off.*

Saturday, September 30, 1837 — The ***Jane*** *of Waterford, Phelan, master, from Miramichi, bound for Cardiff, states to have been wrecked on Fish Island, has been got off without material damage and is now at anchor in Richmond Bay, deserted by the crew.*

Saturday, October 7, 1837 — The ***Aimwell****, Wood, of Miramichi, from Richibucto, on a fishing voyage, was wrecked near St. Peter's, P.E. Island, on the 13th ultimo. Crew saved.*

Saturday, October 14th, 1837 — The ship, ***Isabella****, Auld, from Pictou for Greenock went ashore on the 30th September at Sandy Point, Isle Madame — vessel bilged and will be lost, cargo and materials expected to be saved.*

Saturday, November 11, 1837 — The ***Ploughboy****, Prout, from St. John's Newfoundland, bound to Richmond Bay, is reported to be on shore, near Stanhope, Covehead, but is likely to get off without sustaining any material injury.*

Saturday, November 18, 1837 — The ***Three Sisters****, Burke, from Mirimichi, for St. John's, Newfoundland, is on shore at Egmont Bay.*

Saturday, November 25, 1837—- The ***Three Sisters****, Burke, which went on shore at Egmont Bay, on the 4th inst., has since been got off, with the loss of her lower anchor, and part of her cargo (lumber) thrown overboard.*

The ***Greyhound****, 70 tons burthen, Landris, master, from Quebec, bound for Richibucto, was wrecked near the West Cape, on the 15th instant — crew, and the principal part of the cargo, consisting of beef, pork, flour, bread, etc., saved.*

The ***Two Farmers****, John Mackay, master and owner, from Richmond Bay, bound for Chaleur Bay, was totally lost on the eastern shoal at the entrance of New London Harbour on the 7th inst., together with her cargo consisting of grain, potatoes, beef, etc. Crew saved.*

A shallop, name unknown, about 40 tons burthen, was on shore at the West Cape on the 15th inst., with loss of rudder.

Saturday, June 30, 1838 — The barque, ***Sir Archibald Campbell****, Tait, from Miramichi for Sunderland, struck on the reef off North Cape, Prince Edward Island, on the evening of Sunday the 17th inst., and has since been condemned to be sold. The crew having landed soon after she struck, returned to the wreck next morning, when they found that during their absence she had been plundered by an American fishing vessel, which they observed leaving the wreck. In the cabin, the lockers had been broken open, and all the provisions, and nearly everything portable, carried off. The depredators also took away the barque's hausers, part of the rigging, two new sails and the jolly boat.*

Saturday, September 22, 1838 — The Schooner ***Eliza,*** *burthen 36 tons, Alex Cantley, master, from Pictou, bound to Miramichi, was driven on the bar at Egmont Bay, about ten o'clock on the evening of the 13th inst. Crew and passengers (four in number) saved. The cargo will be saved, consisting of coal, butter and sheep. The wreck is advertised to be sold.*

Saturday, November 24, 1838 — A schooner belonging to Mr. Harper, loaded with fish, butter, oats, etc., went on shore on the 12th inst. at Mimenigish, near the North Cape. Crew saved, but vessel and cargo entirely lost.

The ***Castalia,*** *Barrat, sailed from Bedeque on the 16th inst., and was on shore in Bedeque Bay on the day following, during a violent gale, where she now lies embedded 4 1/2 feet in the sand. The Hull, Cargo and Materials are advertised to be sold — see advertisement.*

Auction

(For the benefit of all concerned)

By S. Desbrisey

On Thursday, the 29th instant, at Ten o'clock, in the forenoon, the

Hull and Materials

of the Barque Castalia, 377 tons burthern, J. Barratt, Master, where she now lies stranded, between Graham Head and Indian Point, in Bedeque Bay; also the

Cargo

of the said vessel consisting of

110 Tons Birch Timber
440 " Tons Pine Timber
380 Three-inch Deals
13 Fathoms? Lathwood

Charlottetown, November 21st, 1838

Saturday, December 1, 1838 — The Brig. ***Clio,*** *Dobson, Master, from Miramici, bound for London, with a cargo of deals, having been cut by the ice, and driven out of Miramichi River, became waterlogged, and went on shore at Stanhope, on the North side of this Island, on the night of Friday the 23rd inst. Crew saved. The cargo, it is expected, will also be saved.*

Saturday, December 8, 1838 — The ***Christy****, Palmer, of New London, was driven on shore in Richmond Bay from her moorings, on Wednesday, the 28th ult., by the ice, and has since been condemned and sold.*

Saturday, December 22, 1838 A Card

The officer and crew of the Brig ***Clio****, laterly wrecked off Stanhope (Covehead), deem it their duty publicly to acknowledge the kindness they experienced from several families in that neighbourhood; and in doing so they cannot too warmly express their gratitude to Messrs. James Curtis, — Lawson, David Lawson, William Lawson and Neil Shaw, in particular for their humane and benevolent conduct towards them. Circumstances do not permit them, at present, to make any further return for the praiseworthy and many conduct manifested towards them, but should it, at any future period, be in their power to do so, it will afford each and all of them the highest gratification. In conclusion, they have only to say, that until their last moments, will they ever retain in their minds, a lively recollection of the praiseworthy conduct of the people of Stanhope and its vicinity.*

E. Brown, Mate
Chas. Cobhani, 2nd Mate
R. Elder, Carpenter
Stanhope, (Covehead),
December 18, 1838

Saturday, May 11, 1839 — The Barque ***Castalia****, which was stranded in Bedeque Bay last fall with a cargo of 400 tons of timber on board, was carried off by the ice on the 18th ult. After having drifted in a field of ice twenty miles to the westward of West Cape, she was brought into Charlottetown on the 8th inst.*

Saturday, June 29, 1839 — The Brigantine ***Charlotte****, belonging to Mr. H.J. Furneaux, from St. John's, Newfoundland, bound to Miramichi, in ballast, went on shore in a thick fog, on Saturday the 22nd inst. at 2 a.m. at Tignish, near the North Cape. Every exertion on the part of the crew, aided by a party from the shore, was unavailing, as in consequence of a heavy gale on the land, they were unable to get her off. The sea beat heavily over during the night, and it was not until the next day that the crew were enabled to effect a landing. A survey having been held upon her,* *she has been condemned, and ordered to be sold for the benefit of all concerned.*

Saturday, August 3, 1839 — On the 30th ultimo, the American fishing schooner ***Twin,*** *of Boston, Peter Sexten, Master, struck on Stanhope Beach during a gale from the N.E. Her cargo, consisting of salt and fish, was chiefly saved, and, with the hull and materials, is advertised to be sold on the 6th inst.*

Saturday, August 5, 1839 — The Brig. ***William 111,*** *which went on shore on the North Cape, on the night of the 7th July, with the baggage and a party of the 83rd Regiment on board, from Halifax bound for Quebec, was got off, by aid of empty casks, without sustaining any material damage, and carried into Cascumpec Harbour, from whence she was to proceed on the 28th for Halifax, to complete her repairs.*

Saturday, 14, 1839 — The Schooner ***Two Brothers,*** *LeBlanc, laden with dry fish by Messrs. McDonald and Wallace, was stranded on a reef at the entrance of Colville Bay on the night of the 31st ult. — all the cargo damage —- the vessel lying there still and water logged.*

Saturday, 21, 1839 — The schooner ***Emily,*** *Cameron, belonging to Mr. T.B. Tremain, which came to an anchor off Stanhope, during the gale of the 13th inst., was ultimately drived on shore and wrecked - Master and three men lost.*

The Schooner ***Three Brothers,*** *of Belfast, State of Maine, was wrecked on Peter's Island, Rustico - crew saved.*

The Schooner ***Asia,*** *of Newbury Port, U.S., was driven on shore at Naufrage, on the Northern coast of this Island, on the 13th inst. Crew, consisting of nine persons, lost. The bodies of Capt. Bastin and two of the men have since been picked up. The hull and materials of the vessel are advertised to be sold.*

On the same day another American Fishing vessel (the ***Georgiana,*** *Corbie, of Castine), was driven on shore at Priest's Pond, East Point, and totally wrecked. Crew lost. Two of the bodies have since been picked up. The hull and materials of the vessel are advertised to be sold.*

Several other American vessels got on shore near the East Point, but will be got off with more or less damage.

A schooner from Beaver Harbour is also on shore near Priest's Pond — crew saved.

Saturday, October 5, 1839 — On Thursday night, September 2, about eight leagues off East Point, the Schooner, ***Albion,*** *Tristram Lunt, master, was thrown on her beam ends; shortly afterwards her foremast parted in three pieces, and she righted. During the next day she drifted, at the mercy of the winds, when the Schooner* ***Active,*** *bound to Montreal, took the Master and seven men off the deck and landed them at Rustico, on Sunday evening last. —* ***Gazette.***

Saturday, October 26, 1839 — The Schooner ***Lively,*** *M. Cummings, Master, from Rustico for Halifax, with fish, etc., was driven on shore at Stanhope during a heavy gale from the N.E. on Sunday morning last. Crew saved. The hull, etc., is advertised to be sold for the benefit of all concerned.*

Saturday, November 9, 1839 — The Brig. ***Montano,*** *of New York, H. Grey, Master, from New York, bound for Miramichi, went on shore near Darnley, on the North Coast of this Island, on the morning of the 2nd inst., in a heavy gale from the N.E. She had no sooner struck than she nearly filled with water, and the crew had no alternative but to take to their boats, and with much difficulty effected a landing through the surf. Her cargo, consisting of wheat, Indian corn, cornmeal, beans and tobacco was landed in a damaged state, and, with the rigging materials, etc., is advertised to be sold.*

Saturday, November 16, 1839 — The new Schooner ***Joseph Albino,*** *laden with timber and deals from Bedeque for London, struck on the Indian Rocks, near the Wood Islands, on Monday morning last, before daylight, during a thick snow storm, where she still remained on Wednesday last when our informant left her. It was thought by the Captain that her keel was knocked off, the vessel being in a very leaky state — and from the stormy state of the weather since, and the low tides, there is too much reason to fear she has become a total wreck.*

Saturday, November 23, 1839 — The Schooner, ***Joseph Albino,*** *from Bedeque for London, stated in our last to be on the Indian Rocks, has been abandoned and with the materials and cargo is advertised to be sold.*

*Saturday, November 30, 1839 — The Schooner **Joseph Albino,** stated in our last to be on the Indian Rocks, floated off during the high tide on Saturday last, and was towed by the Pocahontas steamer into Pictou, where she is now undergoing repairs.*

1840

FIRST STEAMER ARRIVES

In or about 1840, shortly after the wharf was built, a steamer, the *St. George*, entered the harbour for the first time. She sailed out of Charlottetown, called at Pictou and Summerside and went as far as Miramichi. This was the beginning of traffic between Charlottetown and Summerside, and this steam communication by water was kept up, always getting more and more frequent, until the railroad was constructed and in operation in 1875.

1840 *Mary Elizabeth,* a schooner sank off St. Peter's Bay.

1844

MONSTER SIGHTING

A startling animal appeared off Prince Edward Island back in 1844. A monster with humps, a rough skin, and a head raised well out of the water began terrifying fishermen on the eastern shore of the Island. Either the same, or a similar, creature was later reported from Arisaig, Nova Scotia, and it was described as being sixty feet long, at least three feet thick, and had humps on its back which were to close together to be called bends of the body.

The *Atlantic Advocate,* January 1968

Jenny Lind rescue of the *Amitie*, lying on her beam ends, her crew clinging to the ratlines. The painting, which shows the jolly boat launched from the *Jenny Lind*, was commissioned by Captain Allan as a gift for his rescuer. The painting is currently undergoing restoration treatment at the Canadian Conservation Institute (Victor Purdie Collection, Public Archives of Prince Edward Island – 4170/407)

1847

JENNY LIND: RESCUE AT SEA

On October 17th, 1847, the two-masted schooner *Jenny Lind* cleared Charlottetown Harbour bound for London with a cargo of timber. Aboard was the owner of the new vessel, William Douse, and a crew of five. Not long out of Charlottetown the weather turned foul and the little schooner battled tremendously rough seas. The men were almost exhausted when, ten days later, they spotted the Liverpool barque *Amitie* some 450 miles east of St. John's, Newfoundland.

The *Amitie*, running from Richibucto, New Brunswick, wallowed helplessly, decks awash, kept afloat only by the cargo of timber stowed in her water-logged hold.

Disaster had struck three days earlier when, battered by terrific seas, both her foremast and main topmast let go, and she was 'thrown on her beam ends'. Shortly afterwards, a tremendous wave swept away four men. Two others soon fell into the raging sea. The survivors lashed themselves to the chains to wait out their slender hopes of rescue. There they remained for three agonizing days and nights, exposed to horrendous seas which broke over them incessantly and kept their lower bodies constantly under water.

Their faint prospects improved momentarily on the second day when a brig bore down towards them. After a close examination, however, the master determined not to risk his vessel. The anguished cries of the survivors were wasted in the bitter October winds.

The ***Jenny Lind*** *was running under shortened sail when, towards evening on October 27th Douse first sighted the floundering wreck. Initially, he questioned whether or not he should investigate the dark object that rose intermittently in the heavy seas. His concerned curiosity prevailed and he worked the little schooner within hailing distance of the survivors. Night was coming on, and he was forced to ignore their ardent prayers, for he could not chance a rescue in the rapidly failing light. As clearly as he could above the roar or wind and sea, he shouted assurances that he would not desert them. The* ***Jenny Lind*** *was hove-to and stood by the wreck throughout the interminable night that followed.*

At dawn, the ***Jenny Lind's*** *jolly-boat was dispatched to the wreck with the mate and two hands. Although the weather had moderated slightly, the rescuers were hampered by wind, the heavy swell, and the boat's limited capacity. The* ***Amitie's*** *crew were near the breaking point, and only by threatening to leave them all were Douse's men able to convince them to come off two or three at a time. For almost three hours, the rescuers placed their lives in jeopardy, until finally, all were safely retrieved.*

The survivors were in a sorry state. The carpenter had several broken ribs and the second mate had one arm almost severed. All were suffering terribly from exposure. Accommodating the rescued in the smaller *Jenny Lind* posed some difficulty until the *Rebecca,* a brig bound for Glasgow, took off six of the shipwrecked crew. The survivors were reported to represent a pathetic sight when carried ashore in Southampton on November 17th. Douse and his crew were treated as heros and the grateful captain commissioned a painting of the rescue as a gift to the "Good Samaritans of the Deep." The *Jenny Lind* and her cargo were sold, as was planned, and the crew returned to Prince Edward Island.

(The story of the daring rescue of the *Amitie* by the little *Jenny Lind* is retold in the *Royal Gazette* of January 11, 1848. The information above was taken from an article by Nicholas J. de Jong which appeared in the Spring-Summer 1987 issue of *The Island Magazine.)*

TIDE WASH

Those who live near the shore often develop the habit of walking the tide line to see what has been washed in for possible salvage. The most obvious bounty sought in P.E.I. is Irish Moss, the seaweed that is a lucrative "crop" which washes ashore after a storm.

Not so frequent are the spoils of storms which can be alternately horrifying and beneficial. Robinson's Island (now Rustico Island, located in the P.E.I. National Park) was one such place.

After the Yankee Gale of 1851 several bodies washed ashore, some of them now buried at Pioneer Cemetery. In 1906 the find was a little more pleasing, planks and steel washed up along with lobsters, so thick they littered the shore. Residents ate lobsters until they were sick of them.

Over the years the bounty of the sea that the tide washes to the Island shores have brought mixed feelings to Islanders. So often what enhances the lives of one, marks tragedy for another.

1850

THE WASP

The *Wasp,* named because a wasp's nest was found in the hull during construction, was launched from Bay Fortune in 1850. A ship of 84 tons, she was loaded with oats bound for England. With the son of shipowner, Joseph Dingell, and his wife Elizabeth, as a passenger,she set sail in the fall.

All hands, but one, were lost at sea near the coast of Newfoundland. The surviving sailor, Mr. Deagle, managed to reach shore, returned to P.E.I. and told of a mutiny on the *Wasp.* Frances Carruthers, in her Island Heritage column in the *Guardian,* wrote that the survivor told how they would find the crew, one with a broken neck and another with a broken arm.

She says there is a tombstone in Bay Fortune Cemetery which reads:

William R. Dingwell
son of Joseph Dingwell and Elizabeth Aitkin
November 21, 1850
aged 19 years
Unfortunately drowned off the coast of Newfoundland

Parts of this tale are related in the book *Those Were The Days — A History of The North Side of The Boughton River.* The following poem is from that book and was said to have been given to the writers by Reggie Banks of Annandale, who believes the author was a lady from Farmington.

THE WASP
The *Wasp,* the brigantine was lost
And all on board but one
Among the rest was that fair youth
Who lies in a watery tomb.

His name is William Dingwell
His father's only son
In petty harbor motion
Sweet William's race was run.

Those were his last and final words
While clinging to the *Wasp*
Go to my friends and parents
And tell them where I'm lost.

How many friends have I to help
If they were only nigh
If I could speak with Daniel Flynn
Contented I would die.

But now I'm on the brink of death
Where heavy seas do roll
I bid farewell to all my friends
The Lord preserves my soul

1850 *Clausina*, a bark, and the brigantine, *Gipsey*, were lost in Charlottetown Harbour. *Gentleman*, a schooner, went down in Orwell Bay. *Olive*, a schooner, lost just south of Panmure Island.

1851

THE YANKEE GALE

In terms of sheer number of people killed and injured, of property lost and lives shattered the "Yankee Gale" was the event most fraught with tragic interest. The devastating storm occurred in October 1851. Much has been written of the event and through some of these accountings we can get insight on how it affected those both on shore and off. We have presented two versions of the event on the following pages. Readers will notice a similarity of description of events and devastation, but a discrepancy regarding numbers of both vessels and men lost in the storm. True figures will never be known, but I suspect the higher numbers are the more accurate as these two accounts focus on the Cavendish area where 100 ships were reported counted before the storm which left a trail of wrecks from North Cape to East Point.

> *Off the north coast of the Island is a wide stretch of the best mackerel fishing to be found anywhere and many fishermen from Nova*

Scotia and New England frequented these fishing grounds. The sun rose clearly on the morning of Friday, October 4th, and the sea was as calm 'as innocence asleep.' More than one hundred schooners all sails set were seen standing in towards the Island — a magnificent sight — the captains were probably expecting to get their fish in the shallow water; it was late in the season but often the best catches are made then. During the day the brilliant sunshine turned to a grayish sky and towards evening it became black and threatening; the wind was blowing freshly from the south east and about 4 p.m. the fleet started to take off, but they were too late trying to work clear of the land or to lie at anchor and outride the storm. After sunset a heavy swell arose and the captains watched their glasses with anxious faces.

The next morning, what wind! What rain! What devastation! The water was convulsive, the beach a seething mass of foam, the roar was deafening and terrifying. The wind had shifted east and then north; the night that followed was indescribable; the storm continued in undiminished fury all day Saturday and Saturday night. Continuing on Sunday it diminished towards night. The rain and spray had made it impossible for the watchers on land to see what was taking place at sea. As the storm abated help could be given; our sand dunes were a blessing; had our north shore been rockbound probably none would have been saved and no dories recovered. It is impossible to describe the desolation. On the Cavendish shore one of the wrecks was seen with thirteen men almost naked from the buffeting of the gale lashed to the rigging. A waterlogged vessel was aground; boarding it the searchers found 10 men — all the crew — dead in the cabin; in an adjoining cove 14 men, who had tasted no food since the beginning of the gale on Friday, and this was Sunday, in desperation made two empty casks fast to ropes and threw them into the water; they floated ashore and the ropes were fastened to trees by the landmen; four of the men were able to save themselves by this means. Later the hull was lifted by a tremendous wave and landed in the sand near a cliff and the other men were able to scramble to safety.

At Rustico the loss of life was shocking beyond words; one New Englander lost four sons and a nephew, the details are too harrowing. On Monday, between East Point and North Cape lay eighty wrecks and about 150 drowned men. Many ships and men were lost at sea. In the "News of Gloucester," (Mass.), the most impor-

tant fishing town in New England, the storm was reported and I wish to quote from this paper the expressions of gratitude of the survivors towards the people of the Island:

They (the survivors) all speak in the warmest terms of gratitude of the universal hospitality and kindness which they and all the shipwrecked men received at the hands of those generous and humane Islanders. In the midst of the storm they were on the shore to render every aid in their power to save life. After it had abated they cheerfully offered their services to assist in the preservation of property. They bore from the wrecks the bodies of those who had perished, prepared them for the grave at their own expense and administered to them the last sad rites of humanity. Nor was that all, they opened their doors to those who had no shelter, fed and clothed the destitute and bestowed upon the sufferers every possible assistance that could alleviate their misfortune, and every attention humanity could devise. At the instance of many of our returned townsmen our exchanges of Halifax, and P.E.I. papers, are requested to make known to their readers the feelings of grateful remembrance in which the wrecked fishermen of Gloucester will always hold the generous hospitality extended to them in their misfortune.

"Our Island Story"
broadcast given over CFCY
radio in the winter of 1948 by Carrie Ellen Holman

In the July 1900 edition of the *Prince Edward Island Magazine*, Mr. Walter Simpson wrote of the gale, as it affected the village of Cavendish. He paints a vivid picture of the hours before the storm. If you stand on the dunes of Cavendish, and gaze seaward it isn't easy to imagine the hundred of more sailing ships Simpson speaks of. It is even harder to envision those same ships wrecked, the crews dead and dying, their cargoes pounded to bits in the surf.

On the day preceding the storm there were more than a hundred sail of American fishing-schooners within sight of Cavendish Capes. The evening was fine and there had been a very heavy catch of mackerel during the day. It was a fine sight these handsome crafts made, as they sailed back and forth, within a couple of miles of the shore. But next morning the scene had changed. During the night a terrible storm had arisen which continued

After the Yankee Gale beached vessels like these must have been a common sight around Prince Edward Island.
(Julie Watson- photo)

with little abatement for two days, and many of the schooners were driven ashore and completely wrecked and a great number of lives lost. From some of the vessels that came ashore early in the storm, on the sand beach, the crews were saved, but those that struck the rocky coast went to pieces, and all hands were lost.

The ***Ornament, Oscar Coles*** *and* ***Lion,*** *came in on the sand-hills just west of Cavendish. The crews of the first two were saved, but the men in the latter all perished, several bodies being taken out of her after she came ashore. The* ***Ornament*** *was afterwards taken off and repaired, and engaged in the coasting trade for some years. The remains of the* ***Lion*** *are yet to be seen on the beach. I have in my possession a ship's time-piece that Captain Frisby of the* ***Oscar Coles*** *gave to my father. A schooner named the* ***Mount Hope*** *came ashore below Cavendish, and all hands were saved. Further east, at McLure's Cape, the* ***Franklin Dexter*** *struck on the rocks and all hands perished. At Arthur's Cove, Rustico, the* ***Mary Moulton*** *went to pieces and her crew found a watery grave. At Robinson's Island (we now know it as Rustico Island) the* ***Skip Jack*** *met her fate with the loss of all hands. The* ***Liberator*** *was wrecked at Park Corner, and there were twenty-five stranded in Malpeque Harbour.*

The names of these vessels will recall to the minds of the older people many sad scenes connected with this terrible storm. A New London vessel, in command of the late Benjamin Bel, with a New London crew, barely succeeded in weathering North Cape during the storm. They just escaped, for as soon as they cleared the reef, their sails were blown away.

There were about 100 lives lost on the north side of the Island during the storm. Quite a number drowned were buried in Cavendish cemetery. Some of them were afterwards claimed by relatives and taken up to be carried home for burial, but a number of them still sleep in the cemetery with no stone to mark the spot nor any inscription to tell the story of their tragic end.

A schooner named the ***Seth Hall*** *went ashore at Malpeque during the storm and was taken off and afterwards loaded at Bay View with produce for Boston. The Captain's name was also Seth Hall, and he came from Maine. Some of the bodies of the drowned that had been buried in Cavendish were taken up and put on board of this schooner to be taken home for burial. The Captain Hall was a terribly profane man, and the oaths he swore, to say* *the least, were blood-curdling. It was late in the fall when the schooner was ready to sail, and the north side is considered at that time a treacherous shore. The Captain swore with a wicked oath that, "If he got past East Point God Almighty would not catch him." He did get past East Point, was caught in another storm and went down with all hands, the dead and living finding a watery grave together.*

Walter Simpson,
"Cavendish in the Olden Times"
The Prince Edward Island Magazine
July 1900

On October 3rd, 1851, the northern waters of Prince Edward Island were whipped into a turmoil. The waters frothed in a storm - induced frenzy, tossing fishing craft like twigs.

Even as they fought to save their own crafts, seamen paused in their battle when a strange, bright light suddenly appeared. As they watched in awe, the glowing apparition became visible as a schooner, described by many who saw her as burning from bow to stern.

Those who saw the ghostly ship ranged from Savage Harbour to Richmond Bay and many said she was particularly noted as flying a signal of distress which was known to many of the olde salts who had sailed the great seas.

The *Flint*, a vessel from Glouchester, Mass, had the closest encounter and reports that the flag flew at half mast while "in huge letter of fire across her side was the name '*Traveller.*' "

The vessel was not seen again until sighted near North Cape, all distress signals lowered and thick black clouds of smoke pouring from her funnels. The *Traveller* headed out to sea, soon followed by other vessels who took her appearance as a good omen that the storm had ended.

(Courtesy of Archie Johnstone of Kensington who shared his wonderful memoirs with me.)

In 1851, *Bloomfield*, a schooner, was reported lost off Tignish/ Alberton area although the crew was saved. In July 1993, four certified West Prince divers fullfilled the dream of every diver — they found an old shipwreck and salvaged material from it. Speculation is that it was the *Bloomfield.* The *Journal Pioneer* reported on their find, July 16, 1993.

Hardy's Channel — During their first dive at the site (on Saturday), Eddie Annand, Archie Doughlin, David Annand and George Dowdle immediately discovered a huge anchor, measuring about nine feet long and about six feet wide, as well as several five-inch brass bolts. It took two fishing boats to drag it back to Milligan's Wharf and a wincing winch to lift it up to the wharf on Sunday. The guys figure it must weight at least 2,500 pounds.

Tuesday, after digging around for more than five and a half hours, they found two smaller anchors, more bolts, a wooden pulley, a four-foot-long pipe, chain links, a 25-food and a 10-inch wide plank with a brass sheet on it, and a four-foot-wide keep about 100 feet long. They also found a small bone, which they believe could have been from a sheep. It was sent to Charlottetown for forensic examination.

Eddie Annand is quoted as suspecting the wreck was that of the *Bloomfield*, although another ship sank in the area about 30 years earlier. As far as is known, this is the first time the wreck has been discovered even though it is only in about 20 feet of water.

Local fisherman Gary Oatway is actually the one who discovered it last year. His lobster trap lines got tangled in something on the ocean floor but he could not figure out what it could be since that area supposedly had a sandy bottom.

He took down the coordinates of the location on his Loran C and gave them to the divers, who are also fishermen. When they arrived on the site, they saw a strange shape on their depth sounder so they decided to explore further. They geared up and jumped in.

The divers have contacted the Coast Guard about salvaging rights and about possible information about the ship. They would like to have all of the salvage put on display at Green Park Shipbuilding Museum.

LOST IN 1851

The following listing, derived from shipwreck maps and other accountings, is just a partial one, of ships known to have been lost, or incidents, during this terrible year for Island seamen and women.

Alms, schooner of Newburyport, U.S., John Aylwood, master, came into Charlottetown in distress.

America of Lubec, U.S. lost 9.

Arvanda, schooner, off Dean Pt. near Souris.

Balemn of Southport, U.S., lost 10.

Banner, schooner of Hingham, Mass., Isaac Marshall, master, split her foresail and arrived in Charlottetown for repair.

Barbeanne, schooner, Malpeque Bay.

Brothers, schooner, of St. Andrews, N.B., was on the Cove Head Bar — three dead bodies were taken out of her on Saturday, the 11th and another on the 12th. — *The Islander.*

Picked up at Covehead on Monday, the 7th inst. by Captain McMullin of Brackley Point, a schooner call the ***Brothers****, Andrew Holmes, master, of St. Andrews, N.B. owned by Bissett & Holmes of that place. All hands lost. Four dead bodies were found on board which were decently interred by some of the inhabitants of that place. The hull of the schooner is sound and is now lying dismasted in Covehead Harbour. On the Memorandum Book found on board were the following names of the crew: Andrew Holmes, Robert Mitchel, Edward Burns, William Batson, George Trot, Thomas Bissett and Thomas Neil.* (October 24, 1851).

The schooner ***Caledonia*** *(fishing vessel), Joseph York, master, of Portland, U.S., lies near Mr. John Shaws, Brackley Point, advertised to be sold on Friday next. She was cast away on Sunday at 11 o'clock, having lost her masts and rigging, she was left to the mercy of the waves. All the crew safely landed by a rope and by the assistance of the people on shore." — Hazard's Gazette.*

Cambrien, from Rustico, belonging to W. Hodges, Esq., was lost near Cascumpec — all hands saved.

Charlos Augusta, schooner, of Cohasset, Mass., Joseph Edwards, master, went on shore at St. Peter's Harbour.

Commerce, American schooner of Harwich, Mass., John Allen, master, ashore at Tignish near the North Cape. Crew saved. To be sold on Tuesday next, 14 of October.

"American schooner, ***Cohannett*** *of Dennis, Mass., Josiah Chase, master, cast away inside of Tracadie Harbour, near the Niaid Queen, dragged her anchors. She is expected to be got off." —* ***The Islander****, October 17, 1851.*

Cymbria, schooner, off Foxley River.

Duroc, schooner, of Amesbury, Mass., William Johnson, master, drove from her anchors in Tracadie Harbour.

Eleanor M. Shaw, schooner north of Hog Island.

Empire, schooner, Dixon (master) of U.S. lost her jib-boom and had her sails split.

"American schooner ***Fair Play****, Zekiel Cushing, belonging to Portland, Maine, 11 hands on board, was wrecked on the night of the gale, all hands perished. Part of the wreck came on shore a mile east of Tracadie Harbour. The vessel's papers were found and a letter addressed to a person on the Island. Capt. Cushing was a son-in-law to Mr. Morrow, East Point." — The Islander*, October 17, 1851.

Fairplay of Portland, U.S., lost 11.

"The schooners ***Greyhound*** *and* ***Charles Roberts****, of Gloucester, U.S. report the loss of the schooner* ***Flirt****, of Gloucester, about four miles from the Rustico Capes — demasted and water logged — all hands supposed to be lost — 16 crew." — The Islander*, October 17, 1851.

Forrest, schooner, Page master, of Newburyport, cast away at St. Peter's.

Franklin Dexter of Dannis, U.S., lost 10.

Golden Grove, schooner, Tracadie Harbour.

Golden Rule, schooner, of Glocester, U.S., off Tignish. Crew saved.

Guess, schooner, McKellie, master, from Westpoint, U.S., lost her boat.

Harriet Newell, schooner, Thomas Burgess, master, of Harwick, Mass., cast away at Tracadie — two hands lost.

"American schooner ***Constitution*** *of Gloucester, Mass., towed into Charlottetown Harbour the American Schooner* ***C.E. Haskell****, L. Haskell, master, which vessel was found dismasted between North and West Capes of this Island." — Hazard's Gazette.*

Helen Mar, brigantine, off Colville Island.

Henry Knox schooner, of Cohasset, Mass., Perio Turner , master, ashore about four miles to the Eastward of Tracadie Harbour.

James, schooner, off Tignish (a schooner named James is also noted as going down south of West Point) — " *The schooner **James**, a fishing vessel of Newburyport, Currier, master, is cast away near McNally's Mills, Egmont Bay — advertised to be sold on 11th inst.— Hazard's Gazette.*

Jenny Lind, from Nova Scotia, crew saved.

John R. Perkins, of Gloucester, U.S., schooner, lost her boat, had her sails split and deck swept of everything.

Lyon, schooner, of Castine, Maine. Master, mate and six hands lost, five of the crew landed at Cavendish sandspit. (Ships name also spelled *Lion.*)

"**Mantamora**, *schooner, had her sails torn, reports that she passed an American vessel on her beam ends, with two men in the mast heads, but was unable to render them any assistance owing to the loss of her sails and the heavy sea which was running." — The Islander.*

Mary, schooner of St. Andrews, N.B., has been lost on Hog Island, and all hands lost; three dead bodies having been taken out of the forecastle.

"***Mary Lenore,*** schooner, William Dugan, master, belonging to this Island, went on shore one mile to the east of St. Peter's Harbour — advertised to be sold on Friday next.' *The Islander,*October 10, 1851.

Mary Moultan, American schooner belonging to Castina, all hands lost (12) — nothing found but a box containing the Register, case, etc.

Mary Scotchburn, schooner, of Newport, U.S., off Cape Kildare. Crew saved.

Mount Hope, schooner, a fishing vessel of Hingham, near Boston, is stranded at Cavendish — advertised to be sold on Friday next. — *Hazard's Gazette.*

Naiad, American schooner, Queen of Cohasset, Mass., Sampson Hunt, Master, drove on shore at Tracadie Harbour.

Nettle, American schooner, of Truro, Mass, Hopkins, master, wrecked on the north side of the Island.

Ocean, schooner, Reed, master, from Both Bay, U.S., had her bowsprit broken off by a sea while her jib was stowed, lost four bbls. mackerel and everything else which she had on deck at the time, also lost an anchor.

Ornament, *schooner, of Halifax, N.S., James Hopkins, master, is stranded on the sand beach between New London and Cavendish - advertised to be sold on Friday next. — Hazard's Gazette.*

Oscar Coles, schooner, (fishing vessel), of Boston, is on shore near New London harbour — advertised to be sold on Friday next.

Pow Hatten, schooner, off Cape Kildare.

Rival, bark, of Truro, off Governor's Island, crew saved.

Sarah, schooner, Brooks (master), lost flying jib.

Shipjack, *There is a schooner on shore on Robinson's Island called the* ***Shipjack,*** *from Liverpool, N.S. She is loaded with mackerel and salt water logged. I have taken out 30 barrels of mackerel, besides salt and empty barrels; but the worst comes last — we took four dead bodies out of her on Monday last and Tuesday six more, which I think is her full crew.* Extract from a letter from Rustico dated October 7th, 1851 A later report in *The Islander* of October 17th read, *British schooner* ***Shipjack,*** *belonging to Liverpool, N.S., came on shore at Rustico Island on Sunday, and embedded in the sand. Ten bodies were taken from her. She had mackerel on board. It is supposed she had upset.*

Statesman of Newburyport, U.S., lost 10.

Telegraph — *Schooner Cadmus, Elliot, master, arrived in 7 days from Boston, reports that the gale did not extend beyond Cape Sable. Saw a number of American vessels passing through the Cut, all more or less damaged, one, the* ***Telegraph,*** *had lost two men overboard by the main boom striking them while jibing the sail, and Captain (Attwood) severely hurt, heard in the Cut that there were 75 sail of vessels ashore on the Island.*

Traveller of Newburyport, U.S. lost 10.

Triumph, American schooner, of Cape Elizabeth, Maine, Frederick Hanniford, Master, drove on shore about two miles west of St. Peters Harbour.

The schooner ***Union*** *of St. Andrews, N.B., Luther Matthews, master, is stranded near Mr. John Shaws, Brackley Point — advertised to be sold on Friday next. She went on shore on Sunday morning at one o'clock. At 12 o'clock at night she was struck by a sea, which carried away the main sail, the only sail left, she then became unmanageable, and drifted for the shore. On the receding of the tide at day-light, all the crew got safe to land.—* **Hazard's Gazette.** She was later reported cast away at lot seven.

Veloce/Mouraske *— Capt. MacDonald of the schooner* ***Bloomfield,*** *informs us a Brigantine was lost on the North Cape of this Island — that all hands perished — and that she has gone to pieces. He states she was a British-built vessel, 70 feet long on deck, 22 feet beam, cedar timers, soft-wood plank and beams — supposed to be Canada built, apparently four years old. A number of empty Porto Rico sugar hogsheads with spruce heads came on shore from her. The number on the head of one of them was 28 E. 1206 (red chalk) and on the other end 1 / (black paint). The name of the vessel could not be discovered, but the stern of a boat supposed to belong to her came on shore with the name* ***Veloce/Mouraske*** *on it. Her bow sails, chains, anchors and windlass were found to the West of the N.W. reef. Capt. McDonald and others also inform us that there are 20 to 30 vessels on shore, between Malpec and North Cape — and that in Richmond Bay and on Hog Island, there are some 40 or 50 more. It is currently reported that some sixty or seventy bodies have been interred on Hog Island during the past week.*

Vetus, schooner, off Wood Islands.

Vulture, schooner, Watts (master), of Newbury Port, U.S., in the gale of the 3rd inst., lost a man overboard, named Jas. Everett of Nova Scotia; also lost her boat, flying jib and jib-boom.

Washington, American schooner, Mitchell, master, of Freeport, State of Maine, is cast away near Cable head, advertised to be sold on the 23rd inst. (north of Shipwreck Point).

"An American schooner came on shore near Darnley on Sunday morning. Crew saved. Part of the deck of another schooner, ***Windlass*** *etc., came on shore at the same place."— The Islander,* October 17, 1851.

W.R.Burnham, schooner, off Tignish.

Yarrow, brigantine from the U.S., off North Cape. Crew saved.

1851

POPE LOSES HIS PREY

Shipbuilding began in the town of Summerside in 1851. James C. Pope was the first to start the industry here; the first vessel he built, a barque, being called the *Paxton.* The launching of this vessel was a great event, and the inhabitants from far and near came to see her slide into the water. Mr. Pope was one of the adventurers who sailed in the brig *Fanny* around Cape Horn to search for gold when the gold-fever was raging. It is related of him that one day when off the coast of South America he shot a bird. The sea being calm he got overboard and swam for it, but on turning he found that the vessel was drifting rapidly away and he had to relinquish his prey and hurry back.

Pope is a name long associated with the sea and the era of sailing ships. Dudley Pope, distinguished British naval historian and author, is descended from the same line of Popes that have played such an important part in Prince Edward Island history. Dudley Pope's books have been published in eleven translations; his mastery of the details of life and war at sea in the days of sail means all his histories have become standard works. Unfortunately, as far as I know, he has not written about this area of the world, although we did correspond for a time about his family's ties with P.E.I. He and his wife cruise the Caribbean in their fifty-three foot sailing ketch *Ramage,* the same name as the Captain in his series of very popular novels.

1852 *Cyrena S. Colby,* schooner, was lost off Alberton.

THE ICY PASSAGE

Earlier, you read about the ice boats which crossed Northumberland Strait. In March 1852, one Captain B.W.A. Sleigh announced that Prince Edward Island was to be serviced by a new steamboat line, of which he was the owner. He came to the Island by ice boat and left a written description of his trip which was published in the *Island Magazine,* Fall-Winter issue in 1976. Sleigh was a gifted writer who gave true insight into what the journey was like through the eyes of a passenger — who had to toil along side the crew. Space prohibits us from printing the whole narrative, but these few paragraphs taken from the article, may be enough to entice you to look up that issue of *The Islander* and complete the tale. The "nimble fellows" are the regular crew, the "boulders" are huge chunks of piled ice.

> *I found it a most difficult task to follow these nimble fellows; my India-rubber boots caused me continually to slip on those portions of the ice where no snow lay; but having gone head-over-heels half-a-dozen times, I soon became familiar with the ups and downs of my journey. After clambering up a boulder, I found the easiest way to gain the other side was to slide down on my back; this in some instances became a dangerous experiment, as in the gullies between two masses of ice, snow had generally collected to the depth of several feet; and, on going down a rather steep declivity, I found myself up to the armpits in broken ice, snow and water, and Irving (the captain) being near, he snatched at me, otherwise I ran a fair chance of disappearing. This rendered me more cautious in my sliding experiments, for the masses of ice thus thrown together in confusion were unconnected at the base, floating independently of the others around. More than two hours were occupied in crossing a quarter of a mile of this barrier. The wind the previous night was from the northward and eastward, which drove over the bergs towards the New Brunswick shore, and having blown a gale, the masses were thrown with violence one on another, assuming every fantastic shape the imagination can conceive.*
>
> *On reaching the last ridge, we had an opportunity of again looking out upon the Straights. Further than the eye could see were enormous fields of ice, with black patches and streaks here and there, appearing like ink from the contract with the whiteness around: this was the water. A snowdrift soon obscured the horizon, but passing away to the south, we lost no time in launching the boat into a surging mass of broken drift-ice. The pilotage through this was most difficult: all hands were engaged with boat-hooks, paddles, and oars, in shoving away one block, drawing on towards another, or with united strength punishing some larger obstruction to one side. When we would come to a patch of field-ice, one by one we stepped on the frozen surface. A long line was laid hold of, and thus we would drag the boat on the field, and again harnessing ourselves to the gunwales, drag it towards another opening. The boat was shoved, bows into the water, and then drawn alongside the ice.*

Sleigh went on to describe one of the most perilous aspects of the journey; the effect of the tides and winds upon their progress.

> *In we all stepped; by renewed exertions similar to the last, we succeeded in making a few hundred yards of distance, but frequently not in our right course, as the noon tide, which set in with a strong southerly force, had carried us a couple of miles too far to that quarter, as our direction was east by north. To regain our lost ground, we had to make for larger fields of ice, and hauling the boat on it, head up at a rapid canter. It was a strange feeling, when drawing the ice-boat along the runners, and proceeding at the rate of three miles an hour, to know that the field upon which we stood was passing with the current away to the south at the rate of five miles an hour. Thus were propelling the boat northeast, while the tide was carrying us towards the southwest. The experience of the conductors of the boat is here called into active requisition, as what with snowdrifts and the banks of icebergs on either side, the horizon is frequently obscured to a circle of perhaps a quarter of a mile in extent. The compass will show the position and course, but the travelling masses of ice put all calculations out of the question; and the knowledge of the tide's tremendous power on the floating fields, upon whose treacherous surface the traveller entrusts himself, confuses, perplexes, and frequently causes serious doubts as to the real position of the boat.*

1853 *Rose,* bark, was lost near Rustico Island.

1862 *Star of the East,* a schooner, was lost off Wood Islands.

1853

THE LOSS OF THE *FAIRY QUEEN*

The shipwreck of the *Fairy Queen* in Northumberland Strait, on October 7, 1853, was probably one of the most publicized and discussed disasters to befall the Island. Passengers were deserted by the crew, who took the only boat, and several perished. There were even reports of ghostly apparitions, or forerunners, of women passengers who drowned appearing in a Charlottetown church. That tale which is recorded in my book, *Ghost Stories & Legends of Prince Edward Island* will be ignored for now in favour of excerpts which describe the incidents. There is so much information about the events before, during and after this wreck, including transcripts of public meetings to debate the guilt of the owner, master and crew, that it could be the basis of a book of its own.

On the seventh of October, 1853, a sad catastrophe took place in the loss of the steamer **Fairy Queen***. The boat left Charlottetown on a Friday forenoon. Shortly after getting clear of Point Prim, the vessel shipped at sea which broke open the gangways. When near Pictou Island the tiller-rope broke, and another heavy sea was shipped. The rope was, with the assistance of some of the passengers, spliced; but the vessel moved very slowly. The captain and some of the crew got into a boat and drifted away, regardless of the fate of the female passengers. Among the passengers were Mr. Martin I. Wilkius, of Pictou, Mr. Lydiard, Mr. Pineo, Dr. McKenzie, and others. After having been subjected to a series of heavy seas, the upper deck, abaft the funnel, separated from the main body of the vessel, and providentially constituted an admirable raft, by which a number of the passengers were saved, among whom were Messrs. Wilkins, Lydiard,, and Pineo, who landed on the north side of Merigomish Island, after eight hours of exposure to the storm and cold. Dr. McKenzie, — an excellent young man — other two males and four females, perished.*

History of Prince Edward Island
by Duncan Campbell — 1875
(obtained from the rare book department,
McGill University Libraries).

The following evidence, taken before the magistrates of Pictou, after Captain Bulyea's examination, is of interest. The testimony of Trainor, the mate, most assuredly convicts him of the criminal act of letting go the painter of the boat and thereby leaving the passengers on the wreck to their melancholy fate.

Patrick Trainer does not know whether she made any water before the wheel-ropes broke, but after they cast anchor they had to bail with buckets He worked some time at this and then went on deck and began to lower away one of the boats. When the boat was down he and one of the clerks jumped in. After they were in the mail bags were thrown in, he thinks by the captain. Did not see them, but heard them fall down by him, and stooped down and put them away. The boat was dropped astern and he remained in her. When she was hauled up again and the Captain fell into her, he, Trainor, had hold of the painter. The captain took it, and Trainor feared he would have her staved to pieces. He told the Captain to go aft, he Trainor, lost hold of the painter, and the boat drifted off. Does not know whether the hands tried to pull back to the steamer. He did not, but tried to get her away. He would not have gone back alongside for five hundred pound, nor for all Pictou. His life was as much to him as any other person's.

James Webster, called, said he was second engineer. The engine was in a pretty good state. The boilers were leaky, but answered very well. A fortnight or three weeks ago the steamer was aground at Shediac. Has made water since that from being strained, but the engine pumps were sufficient to keep her dry. The wheel ropes broke once before — perhaps six weeks ago. They were not replaced by new ones. After the ship had become unmanageable he went into the ladies' cabin. One of them was completing her dressing. The others were on their knees at prayer. One of them asked him to go to her trunk and take care of some money in it. He told her not to mind her money. They asked whether the danger was great. He told them they were in danger but hoped all would soon be right again. He got into the boat about five minutes after this. Does not know whether any of the officers tried to get the ladies into the boats. After the boats were off he heard some gentlemen cry out: 'Can't you come back and save the ladies.' Wilkins called and asked him to come and save him. But they could not pull up again. Had to keep the boat headed to the wind and pull for shore.

The following testimony, given by Mr. Lydiard, portrays in a more vivid light the cruel and heartless conduct of the officers and crew towards the poor passengers than any other before given. I quote from the *Eastern Chronicle*:

The steamer left Charlottetown between 11 and 12 o'clock Friday. When, after getting clear of Point Prim, the steamer shipped a sea which broke open the gangway and did some other slight damage.

With the exception they had proceeded very comfortably for nearly five hours, at which time they were near Pictou Island, when the tiller rope broke, and the boat immediately broached to, and shipped another sea. Some of the passengers immediately laid hold and assisted the mate and others to splice it. It was made fast by knotting it, but had to be untied again and fastened further aft in consequence of the knot having been placed too far forward to admit the proper working of the wheel. An attempt was made to get her fore the wind with the jib, but she would not work, owing to her peculiar build. After the tiller-rope was repaired the vessel was again got under way on her course, but she appeared to go very slowly: the passengers were not aware of the cause neither were they aware of any danger for some time afterwards. On enquiry they were informed that the engineers were not able to get up steam, and hearing it said that there was a want of fuel, some of them went to work carrying down a quantity of wood that was lying on the forward part of the deck. They did succeed in getting up the steam a little more briskly but only for a short time, when the engines ceased working altogether, the fires having been put out by the water. Previous to the engine stopping finally, the captain, who appeared to be on duty most of the time at the wheel, gave it in charge to the mate. The vessel during this time, and before the passengers generally were aware of the real danger, continued gradually to settle, and broached to frequently. When all became aware of the danger, I proposed to the mate to run the boat ashore on Pictou Island; the mate said that it could not be done on account of a reef that was near the shore. Various attempts were made to get the ship under way before the wind but all failed. At length the passengers all began to work at bailing, and endeavoured by their example to arouse the crew to act with energy. A few of the crew worked well, but generally speaking they could not be got to work, except only at short intervals, ceasing as soon as the passengers backs were turned. The crew appeared to be in an undisciplined condition, the captain having no command over them. The passengers express their firm belief that had the crew worked as they should have done, and aided the efforts of the passengers, the vessel could have been kept afloat until daylight by bailing.

A great deal of confusion prevailed during the whole time. It was proposed by a passenger to Mr. Turner, the clerk, to hoist a signal light, but it was not attended to. After the first boat was lowered four or five of the crew got into it and remained there, towing astern, at least an hour and a half before leaving the steamer. The boats could have been kept there without any difficulty until the steamer broke up. Had the boats remained by the vessel, in all human probability every soul might have been saved. It was believed that the captain was willing and anxious to have put the ladies into the boats, and as many more persons as the boats might carry, and after getting into the boat, on being hailed from the steamer, he returned an answer to that effect. The boats were distinctly seen when they went adrift, and no efforts appeared to be made by the parties in them to reach the steamer although requested to do so. They quietly drifted away — had their oars out, but apparently used them only for the purpose of keeping the boats steady, and head to the wind.

Mr. Power and Mr. Lydiard used every entreaty to induce those in the boats to pull up alongside the steamer and take the ladies with them, at the same time assuring them that none but the ladies would be allowed to enter the boats unless they desired it; and that, if any more could be taken, lots would be drawn to determine who should remain. To this proposal, and to every other they refused to give any answers. All the male passengers could have got into the boats but refused to do so, until they could get the ladies in before them. On perceiving that the boats were leaving the steamer, Mr. Lydiard cried out to the men in the boats, 'You are not going to leave us; — I cannot curse you; I hope you may live to repent of your guilt; but if God in his providence should preserve my life, which I feel assured He will, I will meet you again.'

After being deserted by the boats, the passengers once more commenced bailing, but found their labours of no effect. They got a light upon the wheelhouse and commenced ringing the bell in hopes that it possibly be heard by some one who might be able and willing to render assistance. The greater number now assembled together on the upper deck, conscious that no effort of their own could avail them, and endeavoured to await their fate with fortitude. The steamer at length settled down, with a list to leeward, until more than half of the main deck was under water. Two men were seen floating from the side of the wreck on pieces of plank. Dr. McKenzie and another passenger were washed overboard but succeeded in catching hold of ropes that were thrown them and got on deck again. The upper works of the steamer at length began to give way, something breaking with the surge of each wave, until about one o'clock, and it might be an hour and a half, or three-quarters after the boats leaving the vessel, she was struck by a wave, gave a tremendous lurch and appeared to part in the middle, precipitating all the passengers into the sea, except Mr. Pineo, and Mr. Parker, who were well aft on the upper deck, and succeeded in holding on, that part of the vessel having become detached from the wreck and floating off. Mrs. Marshall was shortly after thrown by a wave on this deck, now converted into a raft, and Mr. Wilkins, Mr. Lydiard, the two boys and one of the hands, also succeeded in getting upon it. None of the rest were seen afterwards, except Mr. Cameron, and it was supposed they all perished. The whole of the upper deck abaft the paddle boxes remained in one piece, and was large enough to have floated all the passengers left behind by the boats. It was composed of thick spruce planks, carefully fastened together, covered with tarred and painted canvas, firmly tacked on, and with a hand railing or bannister running around three sides of it. From the moment of getting upon the raft, so firm did it appear, that they all felt confident of their ultimate escape, and finally after eight hours of exposure to the storm and cold, they were cast ashore on the north side of Merigomish Island, some twelve or fifteen miles from the scene of their disaster.

The evidence of the others was unimportant, being largely embodied in the foregoing.

A public meeting was held in Charlottetown on the 19th of the month after the catastrophe, at which strong resolutions were passed condemnatory of the "base and inhuman conduct of the captain and others of the crew of the steamer *Fairy Queen,* who treacherously took away the two boats, capable of containing all the passengers and crew when the steamer was in a sinking state."

The Hon. Edward Whelan, at the time Queen's Printer, said in the Royal Gazette:

The deplorable loss of life which attended that casualty was owing to the criminal neglect, the cowardice and inhumanity of the crew, rather than to the weakness or rottenness of the vessel. The captain, it appears, exercised no control over his companions, but this fact was not known to the public until the evidence which has since been published, described the insubordination that existed on the night of the disaster. Had there been but one generous feeling in the breasts of the crew, the captain would have been saved from disgrace, invaluable lives preserved, and the painful excitement, and bad feelings, which have since arisen, been averted.

James D. Lawson,
Prince Edward Island Magazine
March, 1903, Volume 5 #1

SHIPWRECK OF THE *FAIRY QUEEN*

This single verse from a wonderful poem by John Le Page, published in a small booklet, personifies the passionate feelings aroused by the incident.

And grimly gales the eye of fate;
The boat is in a sinking state !
The crew insulting from the first,
The Passengers must fear the worst.
Pumps choked ! as useless as the sail !
Their only hope is now to bale !
She lurches, trembles, settles too
In spite of all that they can do.
Yet still they "wage unequal strife"
And work like men who work for life,
To pour the floods, which flow amain,
In Ocean's raging breast again.
But vain is their laborious toil, The leak increases all the while ;
And sink she must ! — but while she floats,
They think of safety in the boats !
'Tis almost useless here to say,
That both the boats were stol'n away !
And the deserted to their doom,
A sudden death ! and wat'ry tomb !
The crew themselves — no lots were drawn !
Have slipp'd the painter and are gone !
The passengers upon the wreck,
Intreat them, threaten, urge them back,
Implore their help in plaintive tones,
(such accents might have softn'd stones)

"For Heaven's, if not for pity's sake
Return — and but the females take !
We're men ! and tho' 'tis hard to die,
For Woman's sake who would not try !"
At midnight black, in such a state,
They are abandon't to their fate !
A heavier lurch ! — beneath the waves
She sinks, to open seven new graves.
Hear ye that shriek ! — but Fancy fails —
Life's battle's fought, and death prevails !

1854

THE ROBINSON

The brig mentioned in the following account was the *Robinson,* named for her owner, a ships chandler of Sutherland. The material was obtained from a 1987 letter from Rosemary A. Rainbird, of the United Kingdom, which is now in the Public Archives of Prince Edward Island.

Thomas Howard Harker, her ancestor, and author of the following, was influenced as a youngster by his grandfather, a seaman of considerable experience who served Nelson at Trafalgar and had his own ship in merchant service. The call of the sea became so strong for Thomas that at the age of 10 he shipped aboard an old brig, the *Robinson,* bound for P.E.I. by way of Bordeaux, France. She was reputed to be over 100 years old, and leaky, necessitating a stop in the French port for recaulking seams and unloading cargo. The baptism on his first voyage did not deter Thomas from continuing his nautical career and he spent several years on various merchant vessels before joining the Army. He lived to be 84.

EXTRACT FROM THE JOURNAL OF THOMAS HOWARD HARKER – 1842–1926

It was about the first week in September, 1854, when we entered the Harbour of Buctouche. We had to take on a cargo of deal, but owing to the shallowness of the harbour, had to finish our loading outside the bar, consequently we were not able to get away until about the beginning of October, and winter was fast approaching.

At last after taking on water, and other necessary provisions, we set sail. It was intended to have a deck load, but owing to the lateness of the season, and prospects of bad weather the captain abandoned the idea.

The weather on the morning we sailed was fairly good, but the Captain's predictions were not far wrong. And before we had got many miles, it came on a terrific gale, with snow; and sleet so that we could not see a yard ahead.

The Straight here was about 20 miles across and we were approaching the coast of Prince Edward Island but it was impossible to know our exact position owing to the blizzard. We did not know where we were until we struck the bottom and then only that we were some miles from the mainland.

Fortunately it was a sandy bottom and the old Brig was tough, or we should soon have been in pieces, for the seas made a clean breach over us, smashing our boats and cutting off all escape. But the boats, had we been able to launch them, could not have stood the seas, for they were already rotten, and would have gone to pieces. It was getting dark, night was approaching, and there was nothing for it but to stick to the wreck as long as she held together.

Our canvas was all blown away, and shortly after we struck, the old brig was on her beam ends and full of water.

I remember Captain Brodick had gone into the cabin to try and save some papers, and would have been drowned had not the men hauled him on deck through the skylight.

There was nothing for it but to remain with the ship, and trust to providence. It was a terrible night. We had no fire and could not get anything to eat or drink, for everything was below, and she was full of water. We had to cling to the rigging to prevent being washed overboard.

The gale with snow and sleet continued until about daylight when it moderated a little. As it got more clear the Captain found we were ashore in Egmont Bay about 3 miles from land.

It was a long time before we were observed by the people ashore. At last, about midday, when it had got more clear and the wind had gone down we were seen by the fishermen who came to our rescue. We were in a sad plight from the cold and exposure.

The captain who was lashed to the rails to prevent his being washed overboard, was in a state of collapse, and had to be carried to the boat, and put to bed in hot blankets when he was got ashore. After some difficulty the old Brig was abandoned and we managed to get ashore and get something to restore us.

I must mention here that I was in great trouble about the cat. I did not mention that when I left house I brought the cat with me. It had been my playmate and companion, and I begged mother to let me take it to sea.

Whilst we lay alongside the wharf taking on our cargo at Bactouche, a weasel got aboard and got quite tame. Singular to relate as the weather got colder it would come and sit by the Cabin fire with the cat. It was a reddish brown colour when we saw it first, but as winter approached it gradually changed its colour, and when I last saw it, it was absolutely white. It grieved me very much to lose my pets for we never saw them again after the wreck.

The old brig was gradually dismantled and broken up.

Prince Edward Island — *We were treated very kindly by the settlers especially those who rescued us from the wreck. The weather having improved, some of the crew went off with the fishermen and brought ashore a good many of the things from the wreck.*

A Mr. Kinley, a land proprietor in the district, bought the whole ship with her cargo or deal. This was the gentleman who took me home with him, and I stayed with him the whole 12 months I was on the Island. They, he and his wife, treated me like one of their children and got me to write home to my mother to allow me to remain with them altogether but I don't remember having any reply.

The Crew managed to get to Charlottetown and secure a passage home before the very cold weather set in, for, so the natives said, it was the most severe winter they had experienced for a long time.

After experiencing working in the woods in the winter (the only time it was possible to take vehicles into the woods) and summer ("The mosquitos are a great torment. They are terrible bloodsuckers") young Mr. Harker was ready to return to England.

Mr. Kinley was the owner of 3 or 4 fishing schooners and a large space of ground on the cliffs for curing the cod. He could see that I was anxious to get home, and just at this time there was a Nova Scotia Brigantine loading in Buchtouche Harbour for Bristol, England. Buctouche was the place from which we had sailed just 12 months previously and was 15-20 miles across the straights and as one of the schooners had to cross to the mainland for salt, Mr. Kinley gave me a note for the captain whom he knew and 2 or 3 days later I sailed with this Brigantine for England.

I cannot help mentioning here the time occupied in crossing the Atlantic. In going out we were three months without sighting land; whereas the Brigantine, the **Orion** *was only 12 days from Buctouche until we cast anchor in King Road at the mouth of the Avon.*

1864

SEAL HUNT

In the early spring of 1864 an exciting and almost tragic seal hunt took place on the drift ice that had been carried in from the open sea by a long period of east wind. A large field of ice had stranded between East Point and Red Point and the seals were easily heard bawling in the calm of an April morning. Very speedily the younger male population of the community was aroused and headed for the ice field, armed with guns, axes and clubs. Reaching the herd of seals the work of slaughter began. So intent were the hunters on the work of killing and skinning their prey that they did not notice that the wind had shifted and was driving the ice-field off to sea. This meant danger and even death to the hunters, as they had taken no provisions, and the boats on shore were hauled up and housed for the winter. To add to the situation the tide had turned and was carrying the ice-field, with its imperiled hunters toward the open sea. Besides, night was approaching and that meant added danger, as their position could not be located by their friends on shore. But fortunately the people on shore early became aware of the danger and hastened to the rescue. They found some flat-bottomed boats available, and with all speed hurried to the rescue. Fortunately they arrived in time to save the imperiled hunters and bring them all ashore in safety. This writer recalls the incident distinctly, and the excitement it caused in the quiet community.

Although many pelts were secured the seal-hunters noticed next day that a Dutch sealing schooner had found the seals they were compelled to abandon, and was increasing her cargo at their expense, but they were too grateful for their escape to mourn over the loss of a few sealskins.

John Alexander Ford
Historical Sketch of the East Point Baptist Church
1833 - 1933

1866

GHOSTLY RUN AWAY

Back in 1866 an incident which happened in Charlottetown Harbour triggered talk of a ghost crew which sailed a small unknown coastal schooner in the waters of Northumberland Strait.

It was late in the year for ships to enter the harbour, when a vessel was eased up to Lord's Wharf and tied securely. The ship was old and weathered, even her name plate was gone. Her owners, it was later thought, planned to scrap the ship, as much of her rigging and running gear had been removed.

That evening a storm lashed the Island, so severe that even the boats moored in the harbour were tossed in turbulent seas. Eventually the storm blew itself out and the crew of the schooner returned, some say to finish the job of stripping her down for scrap. All that remained was a rope, worn through.

Later it was determined that this old lady of the sea had fled from those who planned her demise. She had run before the wind, out of the harbour and away. The next day was reportedly clear and sunny. The crispness that can follow a fall storm drew Captain John MacLean and a young companion, John Finlayson to the shore of Hillsborough Bay.

Through their glass they saw the little schooner, headed towards Blockhouse Point. It was strange they thought, a vessel without canvas and no visible crew. Curiosity aroused, the two men set out in a dory to investigate, and if need be, salvage the ship. They managed to board her, but lost their dory in the process.

The event did not concern the duo. They were certain another dory would be found aboard the schooner. Changing the course of the schooner away from the shoals of the shore and towards deep water, Finlayson and MacLean began to search the vessel. Imagine their dismay when they learned she had been stripped. All that could be found was a torn and shredded piece of canvas; otherwise there was nary a man nor a piece of helpful equipment.

The small piece of sail was set and the two worked furiously to bring the vessel back to harbour. It was to no avail. An early snowstorm hit and drove the vessel before it. The two men were in real danger as the boat tossed in the turbulent waves. Breakers heard dashing against the shore near Point Prim had them prepared to meet their maker.

Fate spared her from wrecking on that shore, but the winds still drove the ship until she was out in Northumberland Strait where all they could do was attempt to keep her head on to the waves. Cold, and hungry with nothing aboard to relieve them; the two men were glad indeed to eventually find themselves in Brule Bay, Nova Scotia. Cold, wet and hungry they eventually manoeuvred the ship into Brule, and again she secured in the nearby mud flats.

MacLean and Finlayson told the tale of their odyssey to residents of Brule as they partook of the hospitality offered. As days passed the people of Brule hauled the little ship from the water and refitted her as best they could. The plan was for MacLean and Finlayson to sail her back to Charlottetown where they could claim the salvage.

As is often the custom a party was held the night before the launching with toast following toast to the success of the coming voyage. It was a wonderful evening, filled with laughter, storytelling and the joy of a task well accomplished; with the anticipation of the adventure ahead adding a spice to enjoyment.

So intent were the partygoers on having a good time, they didn't notice the rising winds which eventually turned into a full fledged storm; at least not until morning. Total amazement froze their faces as they approached the wharf. The schooner was gone. Once again they relied on a glass and were able to pick up the course of the runaway ship. With sails still furled, and no one at her helm, she worked her way out of the narrow channel, around Amit Island, along Northumberland Strait and straight into Charlottetown Harbour.

Finlayson, MacLean and their new found friends followed but didn't catch up with the schooner until she had navigated the 36 miles from Brule to the very Charlottetown wharf which she had fled just a week before.

Unmanned? Or was there an unseen crew aboard?

1866 *Fanny Fern*, schooner, lost off North Cape.

1867 *Star of the East*, schooner, lost south east of Wood Islands. *Lady Franklin*, schooner, sank in Malpeque Harbour.

1871 *Alma*, a barque built in Port Hill in 1854 by George Ellis, was lost in the ice in the St. Lawrence River. She was owned by James Yeo of Port Hill. Also the *Mary Jane.*

1872 *Two Sisters*, a schooner, was lost south of Wood Islands. *Fanny Hill*, a brigantine thought to be built by Edward Coffin in Mt. Stewart in 1868, did not have the long and industrious career he envisioned. In July 1872 she was reported "totally wrecked" during a voyage in the Caribbean.

1882

LIZZIE CAMERON

The *Lizzie Cameron*, built in Souris West in 1874, foundered after a collision with an iceberg in the Atlantic Ocean about 150 miles east of Newfoundland on June 16, 1882. The 375-ton barque was built by James McLauchlan and owned jointly by James Duncan, Robert R. Hodgson and John F. Robertson, all of Charlottetown. This painting shows the *Lizzie Cameron*, a barque, as she was when built. During the early 19th century some 4,500 vessels were built in the province.

(Photo courtesy Prince Edward Island Heritage Foundation, Charlottetown, P.E.I.)

THE AUGUST GALE OF 1873

A hand-written accounting of the famous August Gale of 1873, one of the worst storms on record, was one of the few items saved from a fire which burned the home of North Lake fisherman and captain James MacDonald. The MacDonald family is one steeped in seafaring tradition. One of its generations in the mid-1800s spawned three brothers who all became respected schooner captains. These were James' great-grand uncles Dominic, Angus and Peter. The account was in their house along with old family charts, sextants and slide rules. Written by an unknown hand on the back of an old calendar, this recounting of the August Gale of 1873 was probably written by an old sea captain a few days after the gale. Capt. Peter MacDonald, whose ship was lost when it ran aground on Hog Island off the north shore, was in that storm. Here is how it reads in its near-exact transcription as reported in the *Guardian* newspaper of May 13, 1992.

The August Gale of 1873 commenced to blow about 2 o'clock Sunday morning the 4th of August. Wind in the North veered into the Northeast increasing at mid-day blowing hard. Seas running high. There was a good doings in the North Bay that summer and a large number of fishing schooners were in the "North Bay" so called by the old American fishermen that served their time in those waters.

There was one hundred and thirty-four Gloucester hookers (hand liners) in the Bay at the time of this awful storm. Some of the vessels were fishing around the Magdalene Islands as there was lots of mackerel all around. When the storm came on they all ran for shelter. Some of them went into Pleasant Bay M.I.

About 35 sail came to anchor under the lea of Cow Head M.I. and all broke adrift losing their anchors. All arrived safe in Souris Monday the 25 with the exception of the schooner ***Angus S. Friend*** *of Gloucester which in wearing ship, tripped over and went down with a crew of 18 men commanded by Capt. Adolfis Emery of Canso.*

There was some Gloucester hookers fishing on the North Side of P.E.I. had a hard experience of the gale. Capt. Thomas Hamilton in the schooner ***Rambler****, was broad off the second chapple (St. Margarets viewed from the Northside) when the gale sprang up, in company with another Glouster Schooner the* ***James***

G. Starr (Capt. Hamilton) beat all day Sunday to wind'ard making very little way as the sea was running mountains high, and under three reefed sails loosing sight of the **James G. Starr** *as it shut in thick in the evening. Capt. Hamilton decided to wear ship and run for North Cape. He gave orders for all hands to look out when the vessel came about. A heavy sea broke over her quarter filling the main sail with water. But having a brave crew on board, they put everything to rights. They ran her before it all night.*

About three o'clock in the morning Capt. Hamilton ordered the watch to get the sounding lead, and they did so finding only 28 fathoms of water.

On the dangerous North Cape Shore...they sighted a light bearing Southwest. The Captain says there is one vessel living, the crew all on deck'. "The late Capt. Barniby MacIsaac, a hand on this trip, says to the captain that is North Cape light and you better haul up to windward'. Taking MacIsaac's advise he did haul the schooner off a point standing to North. When daylight appeared they could see the lighthouse and the North Cape quite visible. The Captain hauled his vessel too in a terrible running sea and they stood for West port, and sailed to Summerside.

Their company keepers (the other ships) was lost with all hands on North Cape that same night. With a crew of 18 men the **James G. Starr** *commanded by Captain James Coushin was lost. The* **Charles C. Darne** *with a crew of 16 men was lost, the schooner* **Caria P. Rich** *was lost also on North Cape that night with a crew of 16 men all from Gloucester. The Schooner* **Eldorado** *was lost on White head with a crew of 14 men with her trip. The schooner* **Henry Clay** *was also lost on White head in the Gale with her trip coming from the Bank with all hands.*

The Bark **Appolo** *of Liverpool England, loaded with corn for Montreal, stranded on Hog Island bar, a total loss. All 22 seamen drowned but four and the Captain. The schooner* **Dominion** *of Charlottetown owned by Isaac C. Hall and Sons was caught on the bend of the Island and lost her sails and ran ashore. Her Malpeque crew was saved, the vessel a total loss. This schooner was commanded by Capt. Peter MacDonald, better known as Captain Peter Neill of Souris, a smart man in his young days.*

There was three Gloucester schooners had a hard time of it weathering East Point in the terrible gale. Namely the schooner

__Isaac Patch__ of Glouster was caught broad of the second Chappel at the beginning of the gale commanded by Capt. James, belonging to Cape Britan with a Cape Britan crew. All able seamen, they beat toward wind'ard all Sunday and Sunday night. Making a long leg and a short one, they braved the dangerous East Point.

Early Monday morning the schooner __B.L. Young__ of Glocester had a hard time off the second Chappel also. She was an able one over 100 tons, commanded by Capt. Carberie of Booth Bay, Maine. With three reefed sails she weathered East Point tossing boat and everything off deck. The schooner Arizona of Gloucester was one of the vessels that beat to windward all day Sunday and weathered East Point, coming into Souris Monday losing everything they had. This vessel was off Goose River at the beginning of the storm with a balance reefe mainsail and three reefe foresail. She braved the dangerous East Point, coming into Souris. This schooner was commanded by Capt. Webber of Cranberry Island, Maine, a brave man.

Today James MacDonald and his two fishermen brothers continue their family tradition as sea captains.

1873

THE *FAITH* — LOST AND NOW FOUND — and the *KEWADIN*

Lobster fishermen became curious about something snarling one of their trawls just outside the entrance to Northport Harbour in May 1992 and asked a local diver, Craig Gaudette, to go down and take a look. What he found was the wreck of a large wooden sailing ship. The fishermen, Wendell and Gordon Rayner of Alberton, had solved the mystery of the wreck of the *Faith*, which has intrigued residents for Northport for many years. It was known from history that the *Faith* and other ships had been lost in the area during the 1873 August Gale and from time to time evidence of their watery entombment would wash up on shore, usually in the form of rusted iron nails.

The *Faith* was a 261-ton, two-masted brig launched in Prince Edward Island in 1865. It was owned by Captain William Richards who had married into the Yeo family — one of Prince Edward Island's leading shipbuilding families. In 1854 Richards acquired a large shipyard at nearby Bideford. The *Faith*, registered in South Wales and noted as a "good" vessel by Lloyds of London was carrying a cargo of rails to be used to build the Island's railroad.

The *Faith* was one of at least two vessels commissioned to import materials from South Wales for the railway. The second was the *Kewadin or Keewaydin* built in Summerside in 1866 for R.T. Holman. On August 24 the two ships were tacking their way towards the Northport Harbour with a difficult cargo to contend with. The Captain could not have known of the vicious "August Gale" which had swept into the Bay of Fundy area the previous day, and was now bearing down on them. By nightfall a tremendous gale had developed, with heavy rain and plunging temperatures.

Allan J. MacRae wrote a detailed history about the *Faith*, which was published in the Fall-Winter 1992 issue of *The Islander*, which is well worth reading for good insight into the role of shipping during the 19th century. He relates that as the Great Gale struck, the *Faith* and the *Kewadin* were in sight of Northport Harbour, off the Cascumpec Sandhills. Eyewitness descriptions of the storm provided by survivors of the *Dominion*, *Kewadin* and *Helen* allowed him to recreate the final hours of terror and tragedy aboard the *Faith*.

During the night the storm lashed itself into a frenzy of surging waters and high winds. The *Kewadin* grounded on the sandy bottom and her crew escaped. Later the ship and her precious cargo were salvaged, repaired and refitted and sent back to sea.

Those on board the *Faith* were not so lucky. As it was now impossible to navigate the narrow channel into Northport, the *Faith* was anchored near the entrance to the harbour. It is suggested that tides rose five feet, and beaches were flooded for a full day. Those on board the *Faith* and other vessels laboured to keep the boats into the face of the wind, probably lashing themselves to the ship to prevent being washed overboard as the waves pounded across the decks.

"Some time during the terrible night, as the brig lurched in the mountainous seas, the cargo of steel rails in her hold shifted. Breaking loose from their moorings, they smashed through the hull a quarter of the way down the port-side bow, ripping a gaping hole just below the waterline," wrote Allan MacRae. "Simultaneously, the *Faith* snapped her anchor chain(which ended up deposited in a pile directly below the wreck's bow). The brig's hull twisted. Heavy seas spilled through the exposed hole, sending the vessel down, bow first, pointing north, into the gully four fathoms deep. As she plunged downward, the *Faith* lost her masts, One was swept away, rigging and all; the other fell, broken, into the raging sea and came to rest beside the hull. The brig's fatal cargo, her papers and manifests, her log — and her crew — were lost."

For days following the storm, bodies were washed ashore all along the coast. Between North Cape and Cascumpec alone the *Patriot* reported 33 — some of them likely from the *Faith*.

One of the William Richard's five sailing ships at dock. No date. This could well have been the ill-fated *Faith*.(Public Archives of Prince Edward Island 2815/5)

OTHERS LOST IN THE AUGUST GALE

The devastation of this terrible summer storm of 1873 was widely felt with more than 1,000 lives estimated lost across the Maritimes. Here in Prince Edward Island numerous vessels were lost including *Helen*, a bark carrying a cargo of corn from Montreal north of Hog Island in the area known as the Cascumpec Sandhills with seven of her crew lost. The *Dominion*, a schooner wrecked in the same area. *Maggie*, a brig owned by John Yeo, went ashore off Northport Harbour. She was later purchased by William Richards, mentioned in the above story of the *Faith*, and went on to bring the much needed rails to the West Prince railroad.

1873 *Urdine*, a bark, off North Cape.

1875 *Elizabeth*

1877 *Gypsey Bride*, schooner, was lost off Rollo Bay .

1879

HEATHER BELL LOST

The *Heather Bell*, a steamer, was launched in early October 1862. In 1879 on November 11, she was reported sunk about 9 miles from Oak Island, bound from Charlottetown to Wallace. The crew was saved. Blowing gale at the time.

1879

S.S. *QUEBEC*

In 1879 the S.S. *Quebec* grounded in the area of East Point, but after her cargo was jettisoned she was refloated. Evidence of wrecks can sometimes be spotted in the area, but the waters are treacherous and should only be attempted by experienced divers.

The *Heather Bell*

(Public Archives of Prince Edward Island 3466)

1879 *Mary Kate* and *Star of the Sea,* both schooners were lost, the *Mary Kate* off Governors Island, and the *Star of the Sea* off West Cape.

1880

TRANSIT

In 1968 an O'Leary man, Calvin H. Jelly, found an old book in a pile of rubbish near Tignish. The book was the log of an old sailing ship, the *Transit.* The first entry was for November 22, 1867. Reading the book made Mr. Jelly curious. He wanted to know more so he began researching and writing letters. Almost on the point of giving up, he wrote to Lloyds of London. They were able to give him some information.

The *Transit* had been wrecked off Prince Edward Island near Tignish in 1880 during a heavy gale while on a voyage from Liverpool to Quebec. The ship was built in 1849 by Wm. Clark & Co., in Nova Scotia, for Charles Hill of Bristol. Before being wrecked, the ship regularly plied between United Kingdom ports and North America.

The entries in the log invoke a picture of seafaring in the 19th century. There are reports of fights aboard ship, of men being put in irons (one sailor was put in double irons), for loosing the anchor and, once, a near mutiny.

Marge Connay of Tignish wrote Mr. Jelly in 1971 to say she had the spyglass and dinner bell. At one time they had the small boat which carried the crew ashore. The *Transit* crew remained at their house some time, while the captain made arrangements for them to go home. *"My Uncle Jim, who lived to be 104 told me that he often saw this ships wreck driven up on shore at the Rue and the name on the ship was* **Transit,** *the ships crew could speak no English, but her captain could."*

1881

MAN BRAVES "LOLLY" TO RESCUE *NORTHERN LIGHT*

Thomas Davey was presented with a gold watch and chain in recognition of his humane and gallant effort in the rescue of passengers from icebreaker *Northern Light* when she was stuck in the ice off Guernsey Cover in 1881. The ship used to sail between Georgetown and Pictou, Nova Scotia, bringing supplies and passengers. Sometimes she would be stuck for days while being carried to and fro by gales of wind and wicked tides. Apparently the ship was built to break the ice, but was underpowered and would often fall to the mercy of the elements. Once, they burned all the woodwork for fuel, and had virtually no fuel left by the time nature freed her.

It was quite usual for passengers to leave the ship to walk ashore on the ice when the ship became stuck, often a hazardous journey of several miles over broken ice. There was always a worry of frost bite, losing direction in a sudden whiteout, and trying to keep warm, not to mention the danger of slipping and breaking a limb, or going into the water.

In 1881, the story goes, the *Northern Light* was pushed by the ice and tide close to Guernsey Cover. No one could get aid to the hungry passengers because of threatening conditions of the ice which had been made even worse than usual by a huge snowstorm which had dumped a lot of snow on the ice and into the open water between the ice fields. This created a slush, or "lolly" which imprisoned the ship and made it impossible to walk to or from shore.

Provisions and fuel both began to get low on board the vessel when the rescue attempt was made. Everyone was spellbound watching progress as rescuers placed wide thick planks on top of the lolly, two abreast, and end on to each. It was a laborious task, carrying the heavy plank ahead, then walking on the narrow plank walk. Everyone wondered if there would be enough plank, and if it would held secure. Eventually, the planks were all in place and the rescuers helped passengers in their tentative walk to shore.

AN ICE-BOUND STEAMER

With today's modern ferry service plying the waters between Borden, P.E.I., and Cape Tormentine, New Brunswick, in all but the most severe conditions, and a seasonal service between Wood Islands and Caribou, Nova Scotia, it is hard to imagine just what it was like years ago.

Back in 1885 *Harper's Weekly* gave a little insight into just how our mode of travel appeared to a city slicker from New York.

> *"We in New York do not realize much of the perils that come with the ice, although the East River freezes over occasionally, and the Sound boats have to run outside Long Island, and the people that live in Brooklyn and New Jersey find sometimes difficulty and frequently unpleasant suggestion and excitement in the operation of the small icebergs which swim the harbour numerously, and in their buttings shake up the ferry-boat passengers as fair-sized earthquakes might be expected to do. We present in this number a pictorial illustration of the dangers from ice that beset travel in the regions north of us — between two of the lands that are inhabited by our cousins of the Dominion of Canada.*

"Ice bound in Northumberland Strait," a depiction which appeared in the February 21st, 1885, issue of *Harper's Weekly*.
(Public Archives of Prince Edward Island 4045/5.)

Prince Edward Island, lying close off the coast of New Brunswick and Nova Scotia, in the Gulf of St. Lawrence, is a thriving agricultural area, populated by something like 100,000 people (amazing to me that the population has increased less than 30,000 in more than a century!), who need and are accustomed to a measurably regular communication with the rest of the world, notwithstanding that the ice chokes off its steamers for several months in the year. In the season of open water, steamers ply three times a week between Charlottetown, on the Island, and Pictou and Shediac, on the mainland, and other steamers ply weekly between Charlottetown and Quebec, Halifax, and Boston. But navigation generally closes about the middle or end of December, and remains closed until the end of April or the beginning of May. In the intervening months passengers and mails are conveyed across Northumberland Strait, which separates the Island from the mainland, in iceboats. These run across the very narrowest part of the strait, to wit, that between Cape Traverse, on the Island, and Cape Tormentine, in New Brunswick — a distance of nine miles. Short as is the distance, however, the passage is accompanied with great difficulty and danger. Sometimes, as at present, the summer steamer ventures once too often and too late, and is as hopelessly imbedded in the ice until the warm gales of the spring release her as if she were the Argo *of an exploring party ten degrees farther north.*

As reported in the February 21, 1885,
edition of *Harper's Weekly.*

1881

NORTHERN LIGHT

*The steamer **Northern Light** said an exchange of Feb. 6th, 1881, which left Pictou on Friday the 21st day of January with forty-six passengers on board, including five ladies has been drifting about in heavy ice ever since. Sixteen passengers landed at Cape Bear on Thursday last in boats. On Saturday thirteen or more left with eight of a crew to effect a landing. They got within a mile of land by nightfall but were unable to land owing to a large amount of lolly near the shore. They turned their boat over on a hard piece of ice and succeeded in getting ashore on foot. They suffered terribly from cold and exposure and two of them, Capt. Gordan and a Mr. Pollard, were badly frozen. It is feared Mr. Pollard will lose his feet. The steamer is still stuck in the ice off Murray Harbor with passengers still on board.*

1882

WRECK OF H.M.S. *PHOENIX*

On September 13, 1882, a horrific gale was blowing when the three - masted, steam-powered H.M.S. *Phoenix* approached East Point. The noreaster was powerful, and the westward flow of the flood tides which makes East Point so treacherous were strong. Too strong for the 1,137-ton *Phoenix*. She wrecked on the shoals and other than some salvage was totally lost. The British warship had departed from Gaspé, enroute from Quebec to Halifax, the day before.

*On the morning of September 12th H.M. sloop **Phoenix**, commanded by Commander Renfell, left Gaspé, in the Gulf of St. Lawrence, for Halifax, Nova Scotia, in company with H.M.S. **Northhampton**. During the afternoon the weather became threatening, and the air hazy, so the ship was put under double-reefed topsails and foresail. The night which followed was very dark, with much wind, but all was apparently going well, when, with a tremendous crash, the **Phoenix** went on a reef off Prince Edward Island. The watertight doors were immediately closed, and all*

The Wreck of H.M.S. *Phoenix* as depicted in the October 21, 1882 edition of *The Graphic*. (Public Archives of Prince Edward Island 4045/2)

hands were summoned to save ship. The sailors worked calmly and without confusion. As she was bumping heavily on the reef steam was got up, when suddenly the stern-post was smashed, and the screw propeller dropped into the sea. Thereupon the captain ordered part of the men to construct a raft, the remainder being engaged in pumping, as the sea had by this time forced its way through the bottom, and flooded the engine-room and cabins.

When day dawned, after a weary and anxious night, the sky was black, the wind blowing hard, and the white surf which dashed against the red cliffs showed that there was no chance of launching a boat successfully. Thus matters went on through the day, until about midnight, when the wind and sea abated, and early next day a boat from the shore, manned by four men, put off through the surf and rowed alongside. The crew were directed to lower all boats, and in a very orderly and quiet way the disembarkation began. The first detachment who landed lighted a fire on the beach, and boiled some cocoa for the men's breakfast, and subsequently all hands found shelter in a lobster-canning establishment. The lull was almost providential, but very short-lived; the next day it began to blow again, and the ***Northampton*** *which arrived on the 16th, was unable to embark the crew until the 19th. The* ***Phoenix*** *was a new vessel (sister to* ***Doterel****), and was commissioned in 1880. Our engravings are from sketches by Mr. James Cox, the Paymaster of the* ***Phoenix****.*

As reported in the October 21, 1882,
edition of *The Graphic*

Zinga, a 298-ton brig built in Mt. Stewart in 1872 by Edwin Coffin, was wrecked at Cape Porcupine, Gut of Canso on December 11, 1882. *Elizabeth Smead*, a schooner, went down off Rocky Point that same year.

1882, the schooner *Elizabeth Smead* was lost south of West Point.

1883

THE *MARCO POLO*

I began my writing career as the Associate Women's Editor at the *Patriot*, the afternoon daily paper published in Charlottetown. I was green, a total newcomer to the world of journalism and thus put hours of work into story ideas and just loved the fact that my job allowed me to research topics of my choice. It was here I became interested in the two areas that flavoured my writing from that time forward — food, particularly seafood, and the history of the Island. The search for interesting history to turn into features for my section of the newspaper used to often take me into the basement where dozens of leather-bound books containing dusty, yellowed, crumbling issues of the *Patriot* and its sister publication the *Guardian* were to be found. It was there I first realized that Prince Edward Island's most famous woman, Lucy Maud Montgomery, began her career working for the same newspaper as I. It was one of the things that convinced me that a career as a writer was a distinct possibility, rather than an impossible dream.

There is probably no ship more written and talked about in Prince Edward Island history than the famous *Marco Polo*. It can in no way be

The famous *Marco Polo*, "the fastest ship in the world."
(Illustration courtesy — the *Atlantic Advocate*).

claimed that the *Marco Polo* was an "Island" ship. In fact the opposite is true, for it is here that this "Lady of the Sea" met her demise.

It was that fact that did allow Islanders to lay claim to the *Marco Polo* though. Today she, or at least her remains, lay off the shore of eastern Cavendish Beach. The *Atlantic Diver Guide* for Prince Edward Island and the Magdalene Islands says the wreck lies about 3 to 4 fathoms depending on how much the sands have shifted.

Drifting sands that change yearly determine whether the wreck will be visible to divers. She was exposed in 1982 and 1986 but when author David N. Barron visited in 1985 she was covered. Divers today describe the wreck as scattered. The great mast has toppled and one end is buried in sand. The most striking thing about the wreck are said to be the huge brass bolts that were used to hold her timbers together. One man said the action of the sand at sea serves to polish the brass, and when the sun strikes, it sends shafts of light into the water. The wreck lies within the P.E.I. National Park and has been declared a historic site. There is a monument in the park commemorating the great ship.

The *Marco Polo* was a 1,626-ton, 56-meter, three-decked sailing ship built in 1851 using the wood left over from building other vessels. British author Alison McLeay mentioned her in his book, *The World of the Onedin Line*, which deals with the shipping company history and the personalities of the ship-owning family which was the basis for a very popular, long-running television series in Britain.

We are only concerned with a short few paragraphs in the book, about the deeds of one James Baines, shipowner, who acquired a reputation for shrewdness and foresight.

> *"In the days of flying clippers and their astonishingly fast passages, when a shipmaster might even suggest setting his wife's petticoat as an extra sail, James Baines well knew the value of a dashing reputation. A small man — only five feet three or four inches in height — he was never seen without a frock coat, high collar and bow tie."*

His reputation for shrewdness and foresight stood him in good stead in 1852, when a Canadian-built three decker made her maiden voyage from Mobile to Liverpool with a cargo of cotton. In Liverpool she was bought at a bargain price by Paddy McGee, a well-known and rather shady character who kept a marine store in the city. From

McGee, reports McLeay, the ship swiftly changed hands again, this time to James Bain who had noticed that in spite of her ample beam the hollow bows at her waterline were built for speed.

> *"Launched at Smith's yard in New Brunswick, the **Marco Polo** had massive 'port-painted' sides (traditionally supposed to make the pirates of the China Sea believe a ship carried guns), eight feet of headroom between decks and sturdy masts and spars designed to carry a great spread of sail in gale-force winds. Baines refitted his new ship for the top-class emigrant trade, sparing no expense."*

She became known as the "fastest ship in the world" after making the 100-to-120-day trip from England to Australia in just 68 days while carrying 980 passengers and 30 crew. The return trip took 71 days. It was the Australian gold rush that had caused the *Marco Polo* to be taken over by a "packet" line, the Black Ball Line, filling the need for emigrant ships. She was fitted out luxuriously for her new role, with ceilings of maple, richly ornamented panelling, and stained-glass work. A prison accommodated convicts below decks.

One F.W. Wallace described the ship in his book, *Wooden Ships and Iron Men.* Here is part of what he wrote:

> *On deck forward of the poop, which was used as a ladies' cabin, was a 'home on deck' used as a dining salon. It was ceiled with maple, and the pilaster were panelled with ornamental silvered glass, coins of various countries being a feature of the decorations. Between each pilaster was a circular aperture about six feet in circumference over which was placed a sheet of plate glass with a cleverly painted picturesque view in the centre with a frame work and scroll in opaque colors and gold. The saloon doors were panelled in stained glass bearing figures of Commerce and Industry...The upholstery was in embossed crimson velvet; the berths in separate staterooms were rendered cheerful by circular glass hatchlights of navel and effective construction.*

McLeay was a little more vivid in his descriptions. He referred to the stained glass doors as "glowing" and said of them, "Baines knew where his best interests lay" referring to the allegorical figures of Commerce and Industry. He also noted that a large table made of thick plate-glass lay in the centre of the impressive saloon, serving as a skylight for the sleeping accommodation below.

With all this magnificence to offer, Baines pulled no punches in his advertising: 'It is the largest vessel ever dispatched from Liverpool to Australia,' trumpeted the sailing-bill, ' and is expected to sail as fast as any ship afloat.'

Thanks to Baines keen eye for a potentially fast ship and the seamanship of her master, James Nichol Forbes, ***Marco Polo*** *was destined to become one of the most famous ships in an age of record-breakers. Her first passage to Melbourne and back took the unbelievable time of five months and twenty-one days; the story is told that Baines, informed by one of the dock-workers that his ship had returned to the Mersey, refused to believe it was true until he had seen her with his own eyes.*

Captain Forbes, whose modesty was not a strong point, brought his ship into the river sporting a canvas banner slung between her masts which read 'The Fastest Ship in the World.' In her cabin ***Marco Polo*** *carried gold dust worth £100,000 and a 340 oz nugget, a gift from the colony of Victoria to the Queen.*

The title of fastest ship remained with the ***Marco Polo*** as she made six voyages from Mersey, England to Australia, all in less than six months. Then, on her seventh voyage, she collided with an iceberg; and thereafter gradually trailed out of the clipper packet trade.

There are a few details about those voyages to the other side of the world, which came from radio broadcasts given by Carrie Ellen Holman on CFCY during the winter of 1948 and later recorded in her book *Our Island Story*.

"With Captain James Forbes in command she beat the new steamer ***Austrialia*** *by a week in sailing from Liverpool to Melbourne in 68 days, her best day's run on the voyage being 364 miles...on her first trip she carried 930 passengers and a crew of 80 men. On her second trip she brought back 280,000 pounds worth of gold dust."*

For 15 years she ran people and trade goods between England and Australia for the Blackpool Line before being bought by a Norwegian company that used her for the Quebec timber trade. Water-soaked and stained, she went into tramping.

On July 25, 1883, while carrying a cargo of lumber from Quebec to London she ran aground at Cavendish Beach only 300 yards from shore. Eyewitness' said it was a magnificent, if horrifying, sight to see the ship, in full sail heading straight towards the shore, seemingly with the power of a great locomotive. Her crew could be seen in the rigging, frantically trying to drop the wind-filled sails and stop the rush to doom. As it was they cut the rigging just as she struck.

"...the foremast and the huge iron mainmast went over with a crash that could be heard for miles above the roaring of the storm! Then the ship broached to and lay there with the waves breaking over her," wrote Lucy Maud Montgomery in an article published in the *Montreal Magazine* in 1891. The beach was lined with citizens from nearby Cavendish who had flocked to the shore when they heard of the ship in trouble. They watched in horror as the crew attempted to leave the vessel. Experience had taught them about the dangers of the storm-tossed waters. Finally a sign was made, with huge letters telling the crew to stay aboard ship until the going was not as hazardous.

They waited and the next day were brought safely to shore. The captain and crew were boarded with the citizens of Cavendish for a time. Being of many nationalities and generally of fun-loving character, they were taken into the hearts of their rescuers.

The wreck was sold where she lay, but before the salvage job was completed she unexpectedly broke up. The storm that broke the great ships back was almost as great as that drove her on to shore. The boat and much of her cargo was lost. Flotsam and jetsam littered the shore, and it was said that some $10,000 in copper, coin and goods went to the bottom. It is well noted that many artifacts or mementoes from the *Marco Polo* ended up in Island homes; some, such as the figurehead, later went to Saint John where she was built.

The father of a young man who had watched from shore when the *Marco Polo* met her doom was awarded the contract of salvaging the cargo and dismantling the ship. They found among the broken pieces of hull, beautiful wood carvings and a profusion of brass work in the cabins. In a state room, there were ring bolts and shackles in the floor; and in another room were brackets of old muskets, pistols and cutlasses, most of which found their way to neighbouring farmhouses.

Carrie Ellen Holman related some details of the ship carvings and figurines — remember this was written in 1948!

After 32 years on the sea making history the ***Marco Polo*** *returned to the Maritimes to rest her bones on the beach at Cawnpore, Cavendish. Mr. G.H. Bell, of Summerside and his brother Captain Harry Bell watched her from their ship with a telescope, as she approached the shore and ran aground in hazy weather. Mr. Bell tells me that across the bow were two carved reclining figures of Marco Polo with an elephant standing between them and that the figurehead under the bow sprit was in the form of a woman. Of all the things that must have been salvaged from this famous ship we know of only two treasures: one of the Marco Polo figures, which was for years nailed to the wall of Mr. John Johnstone's barn at Long River, was given by him to Mr. F.E. Holman of Saint John for the Historical Museum there; the other is the elephant which was found in a woodpile, badly defaced and mutilated. It was "too hard to chop up" and so was salvaged. It had been beautifully restored and Chief Justice Thane A. Campbell has it hanging on the wall of his dining room in Stanley.*

Ms. Holman later received a letter from R.K. Clements of Montague saying he had other figures of Marco Polo in his office.

Barron says the site was forgotten until it was discovered by Tommy Gallant of Stanley Bridge. Today, when exposed, the Marco Polo exhibits a number of large brass pins and provides as excellent habitat for small fish and lobster, making it an ideal diving site.

He suggests to contact local guides if you wish to find the wreck.

There is much interest in the *Marco Polo* today and movements are afoot to rebuild, or at least honour her in some way in Saint John, New Brunswick, where she was built. A project headed by Allan Hutton, a naval architect, and Barry Ogden, a high school teacher, with a passion for the clipper ship, is looking at building a replica of the vessel. Those involved in the project say that New Brunswick sweat and timber gave birth to the *Marco Polo*, but her heart belonged to the open sea, and the rest of her legacy to the world.

In Australia some see in the vessel the same kind of significance that the immigration station on Partridge Island has in North America. Hundreds of thousands of Australians can trace their roots back to those who came from the other end of the world on her decks.

Down under, Ogden's project has sparked the interest of the Shiplovers' Society of Victoria, a volunteer group who since 1965 have operated an historic seaport village in Melbourne. They look forward to the day when the *Marco Polo II* graces the waters of Port Phillip Bay and anchors off Melbourne.

If the project does go ahead, there is much question about the possibility of building an exact replica which would be able to repeat her feats of speed.

Sea historians still argue about whether it was the bent keel which came about accidentally during the launching that made her so fast, or whether it was the tenacity of the captain, who had his men placed in police custody in Australia to prevent desertion — or so the story goes!

Then again it could have been the skill of her builder, James Smith. Smith was an interesting man born on the family's way home to Ireland from the Napoleonic War. His father was a soldier, and in those times it was not uncommon for the men to take their wives with them when they went off to battle. At 17, Smith and a cousin emigrated to North America, bound for Philadelphia, they somehow ended up in New Brunswick. He was the first man to build ships in the Courtenay Bay area, and on April 17, 1851, the ill-fated launching of the *Marco Polo* took place.

> *"Her dimensions were such that is was designed to await the spring tide before launching. They were unable to check her rapid movement when she was sliding down the ways, and she ran aground in the mud on the opposite side of the creek then heeled over. Two weeks later she was hauled off slightly `hogged', but not otherwise damaged."*

The mishap gave the keel a slight twist which was later credited with giving the ship her special abilities.

1884

MINNIE GORDON

The wooden bark ***Minnie Gordon*** *of Chatham, New Brunswick, was totally lost at Cape North, Prince Edward Island, on the 5th November, 1884, while on a voyage from New Castle, N.B., to the port of Queenstown, Ireland, with a cargo of lumber. No lives were lost by this disaster. The vessel was five years old and was 640 tons register and was owned by George MacLeod of St. John, N.B. The cargo was valued at $6,000 and was insured for that amount. The vessel was valued at $30,000 and was insured for $25,000. An inquiry was held by Captain P.A. Scott, R.N. into the causes which led to the loss of this vessel, and the court suspended the certificate of the Master Captain John McIlgorm for the space of 12 months from the 3rd of December. A mate's certificate was issued to Captain McIlgorm upon the recommendation of the Court.*

The Islander, Guardian/Patriot
October 13, 1990

1885 *Emma M. Vickerson*, built and owned by Edward Vickerson of Dundas, in 1883 wrecked at Scalterie Island off Cape Breton, October 4th.

1887 Three schooners wrecked; the *Agra* off Seven Mile Bay, the *Jeanne d'Arc* near Cape Tryon and the *Lizzie C* north of Cape Tryon.

1889 *Scotia* went aground November 29th, and the schooner, *A.J. Franklin* wrecked in Egmont Bay near Victoria West that same year.

1889

JEWEL

The *Jewel* was driven aground by heavy seas in the coastal area north of the Boughton River and wrecked November 29th, 1889. She was said to be carrying a load of stoves, several of which are still in the area.

Those Were The Days

WRECK SALE
The hull and material of the wrecked
Schooner Beatrice
of Halifax, 78 tons, stranded on Hogg Island
(East End), about 2 miles north of
Malpeque harbour, will be sold by Auction,
for the benefit of the underwriters and all
concerned on
Thursday, 18th December
at 1 o'clock p.m.
Intending purchasers had better examine
her in the meantime, as the sale will take
place in Malpeque, at or near Breakwater.

Benj. Bearisto
Auctioneer
Malpeque, December 11, 1890

Note: Observant readers will have noticed that mistakes were made at the paper back then, just as they are now. This ad appeared January 2nd, 1891, more than two weeks after the auction was to take place. The advertisement reappeared on January 5th with the sale to take place on January 14th.

The Daily Patriot
June 2, 1891,
price of paper — 2 cents

1896 *Carmeta*, a 199-ton registered brigantine built in Egmont Bay in 1875 by her owner, Angus MacMillan of Summerside, was wrecked at St. Pierre and Miquelon. Also in 1896, *Onward* a 15 ton vessel registered in Charlottetown was stranded at Seal Ridge, N.S.

1897 on August 14, the *May Queen*, 22 ton, registered in Chatham, N.B., was stranded in New London Harbour. On Nov 14th, *Sirius*, 115 ton, registered in Charlottetown, was stranded on Pictou Island.

1898 the *Confederate* lost her main mast in the Strait of Northumberland on October 11th. The 49-ton vessel was registered in Charlottetown, P.E.I. On October 16th *Mary* founded near Mimimegash.

IN 1899 numerous wrecks were reported off Prince Edward Island's shores; *Foam* went down east of North Cape, *Gilespy* wrecked west of North Cape and *Our Hope* in St. Peter's Bay. The *Pioneer*, 32 ton, registered in Arichat, New Brunswick, sank in Pinette Harbour on April 12. On May 3rd, *Amorette*, out of Charlottetown, 18-ton, became stranded at Herring Rocks entrance to Arichat Harbour in Cape Breton. *Charles E. Sea* an American vessel of 136 ton, became stranded at White Sands in May. *Avon*, was found dismasted between Tracadie and West Cape on Sept 6th, 49 ton, registered in Chatham, N.B. On September 7th a gale struck stranding the 88-ton *Lady Aberdeen* of Sydney, Nova Scotia, near Savage Harbour, and driving ashore the *A.J. McKean* at Martin's Shore, between Tignish and Keldon Cape; she was a 83.50-ton vessel registered in Lunenburg, N.S. On November 16th, *Safe Guide*, 35 ton, out of Halifax, sprang a leak and sank 3 miles off St. Peter's Island, near the entrance to Charlottetown Harbour.

"SHIPS COLONIES AND COMMERCE"

Whether it is pirate's bounty or a lucky find at a flea market, some Island coins are particularly treasured by collectors with a seafaring interest, for they have their own unique links with the sea.

Back in 1899 one Edward Bayfield was extolling the benefits of the Island as one of the best places in the world in which to make a collection of coins.

"Everything in the shape of a coin, irrespective to which country it belonged, passed for some value, and the way that value seemed to be ascertained, was by size," wrote Bayfield.

Had anyone been far-seeing enough in those days to diligently collect all the unusual coins that he or she could, a small fortune might be realized upon their sale.

One of those early coins, was a copper halfpenny with a "ship" on one side and "ships colonies and commerce" written on the reverse. If the flag flying at the stern of the three- masted ship showed the crosses of the Union Jack, then Bayfield said the hopes of the collector would be doomed to disappointment and the penny worth only a cent or two in 1899. On the other hand, if the flag is perfectly plain, then in 1899 you may have obtained as much as $20 to $50 and certainly much, much more today.

These halfpenny tokens, referred to today as the *Ships Colonies & Commerce* Tokens, were circulated widely in several British North American colonies, in myriad variety. Prince Edward Island was the principal recipient of these pieces.

The legend *Ships Colonies & Commerce* apparently refers to a remark once made by Napoleon, who predicted that these British advantages would bring about his eventual defeat. It subsequently became a popular patriotic slogan in the British Empire.

RING OR HOLY DOLLAR

Another coin of interest was made so because a shipwreck virtually took them out of circulation.

The "Ring Dollar" as it is known, possesses a local history of its own. It is a Spanish dollar, out of which a round centre piece has been punched. In the old days of the history of the Island, when Governor Smith held his autocratic sway, there was a great scarcity of small change and of coins of all kinds. There were no banks or bills of exchange, and bank drafts being unattainable, the merchants had to send cash for the goods purchased by them in Halifax and elsewhere. The consequence, the silver dollars, were found to leave the Island almost as fast as they came into it.

The happy thought occurred to Governor Smith that if a centre piece were punched from each dollar, then worth six shillings of local currency, the number of coins represented by the Spanish silver dollars would be doubled. The ring after punching would pass for five shillings, and the centre piece one shilling, and the coins being rendered unfit for circulation in any other country must stay for use in the community.

An order-in-council was all that was necessary to effect these desirable ends.

"I am not sure that the Governor troubled himself even to get this authority, for he was one that thought himself quite fit to govern the Island without help from council or parliament," wrote Bayfield.

At all events the dollars were dully punched. But there was dwelling in Charlottetown a canny Scotchman, Mr. Birnie by name, who discovered that Governor Smith had made his punch too large and that the centre pieces were worth more than one shilling. He carefully collected them and sent them to England to be sold for old silver.

He placed his treasure aboard a ship outward bound for England and sat himself down eagerly to await the golden returns. But that bullion never reached the melting pots of England. In mid-ocean the ship went to "Davy Jones" and with it sank a man's chest of hope, a man's vision of profit. The holy, or holey, dollar is both rare and valuable today.

1900

1900 *Hibernia* a 13-ton vessel out of Chatham, N.B., was driven ashore in a gale near French River in September. *Morning Light* out of Charlottetown, 46 ton, also went ashore in a September gale, driven onto Pictou Island. On the 12th of that same month *Fly,* 14 ton out of Chatham, N.B., foundered in the Strait of Northumberland.

1901 on January 15 the *Nyanza* 91 ton, out of Charlottetown sprung a leak in a gale about 400 miles from Cape Race, near the Atlantic. February 6th, *Rita,* 358 ton, out of Charlottetown sprung a leak and was abandoned at sea, 140 miles NE of Maderia. In September the *Opsahl,* 80 ton, registered in Norway, was stranded in the Gulf of St. Lawrence. October 6th, the *Marian,* 70 ton, out of Charlottetown, was stranded on Carey's Shoal at the entrance to Great Bras d'Or, Cape Breton. The *E.J. Smith* out of Halifax, 11 ton, ran ashore on the north shore of P.E.I. on December 1st. On December 4th, *Ste Anne de Beaumont,* 60 ton, registered in Charlottetown, foundered in Murray Harbour.

1902 *Tarquin,* out of Charlottetown, 72 ton, became stranded, Lat. 47 ° 00' N, Long 62 °40' E.

1903 *Queen of the West,* out of Lunenburg, N.S., 46 ton, foundered 23 miles N.W. of Cape North, P.E.I.

1904 *James H.,* 150 ton, out of Charlottetown, was abandoned at sea Lat. 40 °40' N, Long. 64° 50' W on February 15th. March 26th *Elliot,* 327 ton, registered in Charlottetown, became jammed in the ice pack near St. Paul's Island in the Gulf of St. Lawrence. On May 5th, *Rosemary,* 94 ton, registered in Charlottetown, became stranded at Cape George. On August 20th, the *Pelaids,* out of Charlottetown, 38 ton, became stranded on St. Peter's Island off Bras d'Or Lakes, N.S. On October 10th, *Bessie Willis* out of Charlottetown, 99 ton, was stranded at Leslie's Cove, Grindstone Island, and closer to home, the *Acadian,* 77 ton, out of Charlottetown, was stranded in Rustico Harbour.

Broken Hulls are all that remain of vessels abandoned by their owners.
(Photo - Julie Watson)

1905 The *Saxon*, 79 ton, out of Charlottetown, was stranded at the north entrance to Etang de Nord, Magdalene Islands, on June 24th. On August 9th, *Pebe & Emma Small* 70 ton out of Charlottetown, stranded at Grand Entry, Magdalene Islands. The *Samuel Drake*, 68 ton, out of Charlottetown, foundered off Scatari Island, N.S., on the 21st, and on the 29th the *Lochiel*, 99 ton, out of Arichat, stranded in Souris East Harbour.

STORMS OF OTHER YEARS

The tale of the Yankee Gale is standard fare in collections of Island history. It is often presented as the worst storm imaginable and in terms of loss, probably was. However, other storms have created havoc on Island shores. Often it seems these storms strike in the later months of the year. I have personal experience of the stormy Atlantic in the month of November, for it was during that month that my mother and I left our native England to join my father who had emigrated to Canada the year before.

Always prone to motion sickness I made my first dash to the bathroom — and the toilet — while still at dockside in Liverpool. During the 10-day voyage across the Atlantic I spent many hours clutching that bowl, and still recall that the only ease I felt in midst of the retching came from the cool enamel of the tank where I rested my forehead.

It wasn't until we entered the Gulf of St. Lawrence that I was able to leave the cabin. Until then my only view of the Atlantic came one day when the steward lifted me up to view an iceberg through the cabin porthole. A kind man, he occasionally gave my mother a break from her nursing duties by sitting with me while she staggered her way to the dining room of the lurching ship. I remember the iceberg, but I remember more the terror that made me clutch the porthole when he opened the hatch. I was petrified that he intended to toss me out. Actually I suspect the poor man was desperate for some fresh air!

When I did leave the cabin it was in the arms of the steward who had to carry me to a deck chair. Dehydrated, I was too weak to walk. I hadn't eaten for days. My memories of that time focus on three small events. The first was sitting in that chair wrapped in an itchy grey wool blanket, watching the long narrow strip farms on the north side of the

St. Lawrence. The second was a sandwich. So eager was everyone to make me eat that they told me I could have anything I wanted. It was a Marmite sandwich, but my anticipation turned to distaste when the Marmite was half an inch thick rather than my usual light spread. Being proper British I had to eat it, rather than offend. It almost set my stomach off worse than before.

The other was a more frightening memory of being left perched on a pile of luggage near the railroad tracks at dockside in Quebec while my mother searched the crowd for my father. A timid child I was convinced that one of two dreadful things would happen. Either someone would steal the luggage and I wouldn't be able to stop them, or my parents would forget where I was and leave me there forever.

Fortunately neither happened and I never again had to endure as frightening a journey as that voyage on the *Empress of Scotland*.

THE STORM OF 1906

Which takes us back to the storm of 1906. During the early part of November a number of ships were sent to the bottom at the Northeast tip of the Island.

The *Turret Bell* wrecked on November 2nd at Cable Head; the *Orpheus* sank on the 3rd; the *Olga* ran aground near Hermanville on the 5th; and the *Sovinto* ran ashore near Priest's Pond on the 6th.

Pieces of the *Olga*, an 1,100-ton, steel-hulled barque can still be found on the bottom, along with bits and pieces of other wrecks. Incidentally, the crew of the *Olga* was rescued by local residents and housed until they could return to whence they came.

Local people were only too glad to turn out when news travelled of a wreck. They knew there would be lives to be saved and would gladly turn a hand. But it must also be said that many a home in the area would be built or furnished from salvaged material. Imagine the effect of the grounding of the *Sovinto*.

A 61-metre, 1,600-ton, four-masted barque, she was loaded with more than a million feet of lumber. She had sailed out of Campbellton, New Brunswick, on November 4th, bound for Australia. Presumably the weather was fair, for surely no captain would put to sea if he could anticipate what awaited his ship. Later in the day the storm blew up, so severe that the *Sovinto's* cargo shifted and the ship was badly damaged. The captain's order echoed around ship, "lifebuoys for every man."

Attempts to run the ship before the wind worked for a time, but then breakers were spotted by the lookout.

Before the anchors could be set to stop the *Sovinto,* she struck Carew's Reef, offshore from Priest's Pond. Unable to launch the starboard boat due to a heavy port list, some of the crew grabbed hold of the lumber cargo that had broken free or pieces of decking and swam through the crashing breakers. On shore, men ran where they could to help those who were being dashed onto the rocky cliffs. They used ropes to drag to safety the men tossed in the boiling surf before they became victims of the jagged rocks.

I was told that the crew of the *Sovinto* were Norwegian, Swedish and Russian. Only the captain spoke English. There had been a wedding in the community that day, and as a result a lantern had been left on, its light shining like a beacon from a bedroom window. It attracted one frightened sailor who had "came off the ship" before the load shifted and the ship broke apart. It's hard to know who would have been the most frightened when he entered the home, the sailor or the citizens who were suddenly confronted with what must have been a wild looking fellow. His tongue was strange to them, yet they would have quickly realized that another ship had been lost. It was becoming a familiar scene, with three wrecked nearby in just two weeks.

Of the 22 crew, 12 lost their lives. Even though the *Sovinto* was close to shore, it took several days before all the crew could get off. Three men managed to row ashore in a dory. The next night, two more made it, the next night another. So violent were the seas that those ashore could not get out to the ship. They knew the wreck was stable, and that those who stayed on board had six months' supplies. Those who survived were taken in to local homes. John Ryan's father had three at his house.

The bodies of the unfortunates were placed in the coolers of a nearby lobster factory until some were buried at the Souris West Cemetery, and some at Pottersfield in unconsecrated ground. Another report says that some were buried at St. Columbia Cemetery at East Point. The irony was that if the sailors had done as some of their shipmates did, and stayed aboard the *Sovinto* they would likely have survived. Unfortunately, however, some of those who made it ashore reportedly later died of TB. Their burials were paid for by Lloyds of London, insurers of the vessel, who took the cargo.

One lady, who I've only heard referred to as Flora, nursed one of the sailors who became very ill. He was delirious — beside himself —

so she took him in her arms and held him most of the night. A close bond was formed between Flora and the Soviet sailor. So much did he think of her, that he cried when he left.

Later on, children played on the wreck and it is said that rounds of cheese floated ashore. The wreck stayed for years, and even today part of it can be seen just offshore. Consult the *Atlantic Diver* guide Volume III, Prince Edward Island and the Magdalene Islands, for details on where to find this wreck.

> *"Five survivors of the **Sovinto** who came to the city last Saturday gave graphic recital of further details of the wreck, and were presented with an address and a purse of money by the officers and crews of the Dominion Government ships, **Minto, Stanley** and **Brant.***
>
> *Eight bodies recovered from the shipwreck have been buried in the cemetery at St. Columbus."*
>
> The semi-daily *Patriot*

The *Sovinto* has been a favourite site for Island divers in recent years. Ray Murphy was quoted in the *Guardian*, October 13, 1990, as saying he had the porthole from the ship and has made it into a clock. He also has a couple of anchors that weigh from 3,200 to 6,000 pounds, and a few anvils that he picked up off wrecks. He said he doesn't usually take much from wrecks, but did take a couple of running lights off one and made TV lamps out of them. He has also dived around the *Olga*, and took a porthole off that ship too.

As is often the case the stormy weather continued through November in that year — 1906. On the 16th day, another vessel met her demise. *A.J. MacLean,* weighing 65 ton, was lost. The local Sea Rescue Team from Northport and Alberton risked their lives to save most of the crew of the *A.J. MacLean.* A sailor's monument erected between Northport and Alberton commemorates the bravery and the sad loss of life that occurred.

Another hero of the storm was Captain Harry Broom, master of the last Windjammer ever built in Montague. The *J.W.* (named for her builder James Wightman) loaded with salt herring had set sail for Halifax when the storm blew up. Captain Broom read the signs and knew they were in for a blow. Taking quick action he had the crew "snug down" the *J.W.* then lash him to the wheel, before they took refuge below decks. It was believed by many that his brave action saved the lives of the crew, the cargo and the boat herself from the fate that met so many others during the days of the 1906 gales.

THE WRECK OF THE *SAVINTA**
November 6th, 1906

Come all you jolly seamen bold, and listen onto me
About a story I will tell, that happened on the sea.
Was the loss of the ship "Savinta" on the Atlantic Coast
On Crew's Reef at Prince Edward Isle she was completely lost.

T'was on the fourth of November, when first she did set sail
And scarcely had she laid her course when encountered with a gale
Until the sixth that dreadful night, a storm there did arise,
The raging billows loud did roar, and dismal were the skies.
Then from the deck they saw the land, that nite so dark and drear.
They thought upon their native homes, and friends they loved so dear.
They tho't upon their loving wives, who wept for them ashore.
Likewise, a tender mother, which they'd never see no more.

They battled with the heavy seas, those sailors young and brave.
For well they knew, their time had come to meet a watery grave.
The waves came with fearful crash, she drives against a rock.
Then all her masts and timbers smash beneath the furious shock.

It comes again, and yet again, with still increasing force.
Now all the help of man is vain, the tempest takes its course.
The ship breaks up; her scattered parts float on the foaming wave,
And all the crew, with trembling hearts, look for a watery grave.

There was a gallant lad on board. Arthur Gerwich was his name.
Who volunteered to go on shore some help for to obtain.
He tied a lifebelt 'round his waist, and did a plank secure
And soon upon the fleeting wave, amid the deafening roar.

He landed there in safety, for it was so to be,
And quickly went in search of help, as soon as he could see,
And there so weary, wet and worn, he stood at Ross' door
And told the awful story of his comrades on the shore.

Then the good people of the Isle, with willing heart and hand
They gather there by hundred, down by the ocean strand,
But all their efforts were in vain: no help could they bestow,
So dreadful were the raging seas, likewise the undertow.
All night in this condition they were washed to and fro.
At daylight, in the morning they were in the midst of woe,
Then, getting no help from the shore, the captain then did say,
"My boys, we must derive a plan now, for the get away."

"There is no lifeboats on the shore, there is not helping hand.
We'll launch out little lifeboat now, and try to make the land."
Then all these sailors young and brave, they quickly did obey,
And soon did cut the lifeboat clear, and lowered her away.

But hardly had they got within, when she was buried low,
And every gallant soul, my boys, then overboard did go,
And some clung to that little boat, some swam to plank and deal,
And three swam to the sinking ship, some safety place to feel.

And those that swam to plank and deal, and those upon the craft
Were swiftly felled to the shore, there by the raging blast.
And some were killed against the rocks, some landed safe on shore,
And some swept by the undertow where they were seen no more.

Now Austin Grady and C. Campbell stood upon the shore
To see three sailor on that wreck, it grieved their hearts full sore.
They looked around, and yet around, a boat for to secure
That they might rescue these poor souls, and land them safe on shore.

There was a dory on the beach, but she was small and frail.
They quickly launched her in the sea, to face the raging gale.
But there she filled and filled again, T'would grieve your heart with pain
To see these brave young men there try, and try, and try again.

They tried again, and yet again, as both of them agreed
And like a spider at its' web, at last they did succeed,
And then from out the undertow they rowed with careful skill,
For well they knew their little craft the slightest thing would fill .

They rowed out to that scene, and there they hard did try
And rescued two brave seamen, e'er they were doomed to die.
But there was one brave seaman, upon that wreck alone
He felt the cold waves sweep his form, he heard the timbers groan.

For sixty hours he laid there, and heard that mournful roar,
And faintly raised his weary eyes, and longed and longed for shore.
But e'er he sank to rise no more, a goodly plank appeared
And swiftly fleeting to the shore, the drowning seaman cheered.

It cheered his heart, it saved his life, amid the deafening roar,
Midst wind and seas, and ocean strife, it bro't him safe to shore.
So now this little rescued band found all their troubles past,
And safe, and thankful on the shore, eleven had arrived at last.

But ten poor souls had lost their lives, and met a watery grave
So come, all you rescued bank, pray for your comrades brave.
And may God bless these ten poor souls, who met a watery grave
For they were noble-hearted men, likewise both young and brave.
And hope friends and parents will weep for them no more,
And may their souls in glory shine, on Caanan's happy shore.
From the family collection of Debbie Gamble-Arsenault.

Author unknown.

1906 The *Genesta,* 393 ton, out of Charlottetown, was stranded on Alacran Reef in the Gulf of Mexico on January 24th. *A. Lincoln,* 58 ton, out of Charlottetown, was stranded near Rustico on May 29th, and the *Alma,* 65 ton, out of Charlottetown, was stranded in Northumberland Strait on August 6th.

1906

HEROISM AT ALBERTON

The following, written by J.C. Lewis, appeared in the *Halifax Herald,* in 1935.

Twenty-nine years ago today, the people of P.E.I. were thrilled by the news of as daring a rescue at seas as anything its annals can record. On the morning the citizens of Alberton awoke to learn that at midnight on the previous night the schooner ***A.J. McKean,*** *a vessel of 60 tons register, had struck the North Bar while she was endeavouring to make port in the middle of the terrible Northeast storm. A gale from the northeast has been blowing for days, and while the morning of the 16th found the wind moderating somewhat, a tremendous sea was still running. The crew of the ill-fated could be seen from shore clinging to the shrouds. At any moment, due to the merciless pounding she was receiving, the vessel was liable to break up.*

Capt. John Champion of the **Sarah P. Ayre** *who was in port at the time, realized that if assistance to the unfortunate crew was to be of any value, it would have to be forthcoming at once. He called for volunteers about 7 a.m. The men who responded to the call were ten in number, all inquired to the hardships and dangers of the sea, and they ranged in age from 22 to 50 years. The great majority of the crew of volunteers were married men with wives and children, but without a murmur they took their places calmly at the oars to battle with the angry, sullen sea in order that those helpless men doggedly and grimly hanging on for life in the shrouds of the doomed* ***A.J. McKean*** *might be saved.*

By 11 o'clock they had succeeded in approaching on the leeward side to within a few yards of the stricken schooner. Tumultuous seas were breaking over her from stem to stern. By sign, for it was impossible to make one's voice heard against the gale of the wind, they gave the crew orders to fasten a rope to the foremast. William Mallett, now keeper of the main light in Alberton Harbour did so, and grasping the rope firmly, leaped into the seas. Eager hands aboard the seine boat pulled him into safety. Jerome Richards and Joseph Laviolette, the other members of the crew, followed in that order named. There now remained only the Captain, Thomas DesRoches.

Either because he was suffering from asthma and numb with cold, he could not move about, or because his reasoning faculties had become stupefied at the realization of the impending loss of his vessel, Capt. DesRoches appeared indifferent to his fate. Apparently conscious of the presence of nearby potential rescuers, the Captain, nevertheless, made no serious effort to help the seine boat's gallant crew save his life, and in that raging sea it was impossible to put the seine alongside the pounding vessel because of the tremendous power of the undertow. Three times the gallant seine-boat's crew tried it recklessly, risking their own lives in an attempt, only to be forced to draw away, and that drawing away alone made possible by supreme seamanship, leave the blades of broken oars floating on the storm-tossed waters.

William Leavitt, son-in-law of Captain Champion, was a member of that life-saving crew. Courageous beyond all ideas of courage which the ordinary man ascribes to his fellowman, Leavitt grew frantic as he realized that if the McKean's captain was to be saved, something must be done at once. He snatched a rope, tied it around his waist, kicked off his sea boots and prepared to try to swim through that angry surf to the doomed vessel. Yet, sublime as was the motive for Leavitt's action, magnificent and inspiring as was his forgetfulness of self in such a crisis, we must remember it would have been impossible for any man to have withstood for more than a few minutes the buffeting of such a sea. Captain Champion, with a wisdom born of a lifetime experience on the water, refused to allow Leavitt to make the attempt, and he was forcibly restrained by the other members of the crew.

Shortly afterwards a gigantic sea struck ***McKean*** *amid ships. She broke in two afor or two aft of the forecastel and Captain DesRoches, releasing his hold on the foremast, fell between the two broken parts of the vessel. He was seen no more.*

For another hour or more the seine-boat remained in the vicinity of the wreck, but finally, after having satisfied themselves as to the tragic fate of Capt. DesRoches, the life-saving crew with the three survivors of the lost ***A.J. McKean****, returned to Alberton Harbour; they had left about 7 in the morning; they returned at 2 in the afternoon. Hundreds of people greeted them on the wharf, saddened by the news of the death of Capt. DesRoches, but overjoyed to know the lives of the crew had been saved. Shortly afterwards the Hon. A.A. LeFugey, Federal member for Prince County, brought the news of the rescue to the attention of the House of Commons at Ottawa, with the result that the Government of Canada presented watches and medals to the members of the life-saving crew. The Charlottetown* ***Guardian*** *in it's issue of*

November 17, 1906, stated the deed of daring off Alberton Harbour on November 16, was one of the most heroic rescues ever made in the annals of the seas, and we shall leave it at that. The names of those men who boldly set out into an angry sea to rescue their fellow men are: Capt. John Champion, Capt. Daniel Fraser, John McCabe, William Smith, George MacBeth, Frank Skerry, Charles McNeill, Charles Perry, James Tuplin, James Cahill, and William Leavitt.

Alberton Museum

1907 The *Halycon* was wrecked off Brown's Cape in the area north of the Boughton River on November 7, with all hands lost. Another noted wreck was the *Ripley Ropes* (year uncertain).

Those Were The Days

1910 The *Empress,* 26 ton, out of Charlottetown, stranded in St. Peter's Bay on May 13th. On September 22nd the John M. Plummer, 83 ton, out of Halifax, stranded in Northumberland Strait. *Neil Dow,* 48 ton, out of Charlottetown, stranded in Richibucto Harbour, N.B. on October 30th. The *Genesta,* out of Barrington, N.S., was stranded off Murray Harbour on Dec. 14th.

1911 *Laura Victoria,* of Arichat, N.S., foundered off Murray Harbour, date unknown. On July 28th *Axa,* out of Charlottetown, burnt in Northumberland Strait, P.E.I. August 20, *Kohinoor,* of Charlottetown, 77 ton, was stranded on Gallows Pt. Reef in Hillsborough Bay. The *Elva M,* 92 ton, was driven on shore at North Arm Pt., Bay of Islands, Nfld. on Sept. 7th, and on the 9th, *Ladier Naapier,* 210 ton, was abandoned in the Atlantic Ocean, both were out of Charlottetown. The *Electra,* of Charlottetown, 78 ton, stranded at the entrance to Margaree Harbour, N.S. on October 25th; on the 31st, *James A. Stetson,* out of Pictou, N.S., 71.26 ton, was stranded at Alberton. *St Patrick,* 27 ton, of Halifax, stranded at Little River. *Maria,* out of Miramichi, N.B., 28 ton, stranded on Panmure Island on December 1.

1912 *Warren W.,* 79 ton, was stranded at Big Bras d'Or, Cape Breton, on May 19. *Arclight,* 103 ton, sprung a leak and was abandoned in New York Harbour, U.S.A., on July 12th. James Grey, 91 ton, foundered near Magdalene Islands on August 24th, and the *Abraham Lincoln,* 58 ton, was stranded at the north entrance to the Straight of Canso. All of these vessels were out of Charlottetown .

1913 *Irene,* 64 ton, out of Halifax, stranded off Mount Carmel on August 9th. That same month, *Nuletus,* out of Lunenburg, N.S., 95.91 ton, was stranded at Cape Bear. *E.B. No. 1,* out of Toronto, 139 ton, stranded six miles from Rustico on September 8th. On November 1, *Flora T.*, 52 ton, out of Charlottetown, foundered at Canoe Cove.

IONA
The Charlottetown Examiner
January 3, 1914

***Ottawa** — Search for the missing schooner, **Iona,** which left Montague, P.E.I., twenty-two days ago, and has not been heard from since, has been given up. It seems probable that this vessel will be added to the mysteries of the sea. In this connection the Department of Marine and Fisheries is requested by the British Board of Trade to hold an investigation into the loss of the vessel as well as into the disappearance of the steamer **Bridgeport** which was never heard from after leaving port a month ago. Such disappearance with the absence of any indication of the fate of missing vessels is rare in Canada.*

The Charlottetown Examiner
January 6, 1914
"Schooner *Iona W.* Went Down With All Hands"

GEORGE N. ORR

In times of war many vessels are pulled into service for which they are not intended, sometimes successfully, sometimes not. In the case of the *George N. Orr* and five other lake boats sold by Canada to the U.S.A. during the First World War, success was not in the master plan.

The six boats were not designed for ocean travel but the need for boats to perform coastal service was great so this risk was taken — not a good decision it turned out for not one survived ocean travel. The *George N. Orr* went down in a raging storm east of Savage Harbour after her steering gear was damaged about 10 miles off East Point. She drifted helpless before the storm until she hit bottom, ripping open her bottom plates. Saltwater ruined the cargo of hay, which animals simply refused to eat even when it was dried and shook out.

Walter O'Brien, endeared to many readers for his newspaper column "Bristol Notes," once wrote about the *George N. Orr:* "She was resting in very shallow water near the shore, with her bottom torn, and the tide would rise inside the ship as it rose and fell outside. The big ship was there for several years, until it was finally sold for junk. It was cut up in the winter months and hauled to a city junk yard for the scrap.

"It was one terrible November night. A sister ship, the *Simcoe*, was lost and sank off the Magdalene Islands in the worst night ever reported here. There are few today who remember the *George N. Orr* that night, with gale force winds and tides that raced up the shoreline and onto farm lands before it ended."

Today the anchor and other items are to be found in local homes, and the remains of the *George N. Orr* are home to lobsters, eels, and other fish and marine life, and a great attraction for divers.

1914 *Sir Louis*, 86 ton, out of Charlottetown, foundered 1/2 mile outside Pt. Brule on May 9th. On June 5, *James Ryan*, out of Port Medway, N.S., 48 ton, was stranded at Cape Egmont. *Nellie M. Snow*, 75 ton, out of Charlottetown, stranded in Pownal Bay on August 27th. In October, *Emilien Burke*, out of Yarmouth, N.S., 89.76 ton, was stranded in Cardigan Bay. November 14, *Harry B.*, out of Charlottetown, 67 ton, collided with the *Dictator* in Pictou Harbour. On the 20th, *Limelight*, out of Charlottetown, 126 ton, was stranded at Wine Harbour, N.S.

1915 *Uncle Sam*, out of Halifax, 77 ton, stranded at Tryon Cove on April 27th. On June 24th, *Cabot*, out of Montreal, 162 ton, foundered off East Point. On June 27th, *Donzella*, out of Charlottetown, 99.18 ton, stranded at Guyon Island, N.S. *Vera B. Roberts*, out of Parrsboro, N.S., 124 ton, burnt off Victoria on Sept 17th. *John Millard*, out of Charlottetown, 69 ton, collided with a sunken rock off Pictou, N.S., on Sept 27th. *Edward Hall No 1*, of Sarnia, Ontario, burnt off Rocky Point on December 2nd.

1916 *Western Light*, Charlottetown, 38.68 ton, was stranded in Harding Channel on July 1st. *Veeta*, of New London, 113 ton, foundered three miles east of Seal Island, N.S. on July 21. *Hazel Glen*, of Annapolis, N.S., 89 ton, was stranded on Malpeque Reef on July 31st. On November 14th, *W. Parnell O'Hara*, of Charlottetown, 79 ton, foundered in Malpeque Harbour.

1917 On July 16th *Oregon*, of Charlottetown, 46 ton, was stranded at the entrance to Whitehead, H.S. On August 17th, *Cyrene*, of Lunenburg, N.S., 96 ton, collided with the *Aranmore* in Northumberland Strait.

Albert King of Georgetown recalled the winter of 1917 in a newspaper interview for *The Eastern Graphic*, published March 7, 1979. He was 80 at the time.

> *The ice was so thick a man could walk from Georgetown to Souris, or keep on going to East Point if he wanted. Three boats made it through from Pictou to Panmure. We went out with horse and sleigh from Georgetown, over the ice to where the boats were lying off Panmure. We unloaded them through the portholes, mostly fruit and vegetables it was. And we loaded port and black oats on board. What is black oats: that's a small hard oat, real good for horses. We worked for three days and three nights without stopping, as soon as one boat was finished, we did the next. I was so tired, I fell asleep holding onto the sleigh. I was seventeen then and strong, but we worked. Mr God, we worked hard.*

1918 *Sarah P. Ayer*, of Charlottetown, 64 ton, was stranded at Grand Entry, Magdalene Islands on May 30th. June 9th, *Mary E. Macdougall*, of Charlottetown, 98 ton, was stranded at the entrance to Bras d'Or Lake, Cape Breton. *G.C. Kelley*, of Charlottetown, 99 ton, foundered in Charlottetown Harbour on July 30th. *Olive S.*, out of Charlottetown, 26 ton, was stranded in Tangier Harbour on Sept. 6th.

1919 *Daisy*, of Charlottetown, 69.71 ton, foundered in Northumberland Strait on September 16th.

1920 *Alena L. Young*, 35.28 ton, of Charlottetown, stranded on Tryon Shoal on July 2nd. On August 31st, *Maggie May*, out of Halifax, 62 ton, collided with the dock in Charlottetown Harbour. The *Dart* of Pictou, N.S., 44 ton, was stranded in the Hillsborough River on October 4th. *Emilien Burke*, of Charlottetown, 90 ton, became stranded near Port au Port, Nfld., on December 3rd.

1921 *Bessie S.Keefer*, 79 ton, owned by Captain L. Michael Kinch of Alberton, and registered in Charlottetown, foundered off the east coast of Nova Scotia on May 6th. On November 13th, *Howard*, 93 ton out of Lunenburg, N.S., was stranded at Pinette. On November 26th, *Corporal Trim*, 57 ton, of Charlottetown, was stranded at Stewart Point, Belle River.

1922 *Grand Desert*, 65.44 ton, out of Halifax, stranded at Bayfield on May 8th. *Iona*, out of Charlottetown, 98 ton, was stranded at Simcoe Bridge, N.S., on June 24th. *Harry B.* of Charlottetown, 98 ton, foundered near Toney River, N.S.

1923 *Maggie May*, 62.18 ton, out of Charlottetown, stranded in Orwell Bay on October 2nd.

1924 On August 27th, the *Anna MacDonald*, 191 ton, stranded on Kitty Wells Shoals near Prospect, N.S. On November 6th, *Happy Go Lucky*, 36 ton, stranded on the Grand River Bar. Both vessels were out of Charlottetown.

1925

NEVER-TO-BE-FORGOTTEN STRAIT CROSSING

*The great ice breaker, the **Prince Edward**, a coal-burning ship with six boilers for power, was the first one on the route that connects the Island with the mainland. This fine ship came here in 1915 and went to Borden in 1917 after the pier and dock were built. She was a rail-carrying ship with rails on her main deck called the car deck. She took 12 standard-gauge freight cars at one trip and less passenger or express and mail cars owing to their great length. Of course passenger cars were not carried. Passengers went up the ramps of the ship to the quarter deck and the lounge above it, walking up and down. This great ship backed into the dock and became connected to the ramp by an apron lowered by the engineer in the power house at each dock.*

The master of this mighty ship was Capt. John L. Read with a crew of about eighty officers and engineers. Being a coal-burning ship, some four tons of coal per hour were used by the eighteen firemen. Trimmers, or firemen's helpers cleaned up after the ashes, hoisted it by hand winches and dumped it into the sea on the crossings with no dumping in the docks.

One trip never to be forgotten was in the spring of 1925 when the big ship left Borden on its regular passenger and freight about 9 a.m. Saturday and failed to reach Tormentine dock until the following Tuesday, about noon. The troubled ship became caught in grounded ice about half a mile from Tormentine and was unable to free herself and despite all the efforts remained stuck solid there for 76 hours. The ice around the ship was tar black from the smoke and soot from the stacks of the six boilers as efforts to work free went on day and night. Food was getting low and coal from the reserve bunkers was running low on Tuesday morning when the master ordered the ice boats lowered to take the baggage ashore while the passengers were told to abandon ship and walk ashore under direction of Capt. A.B. Paquet on the ship. It was a sight never to be forgotten by those on duty. As we watched the men and women walk ashore they arrived safe and climbed the ladders onto the pier but the strangest part of it all was that a change of wind that morning loosened the ice and the ship backed out of her locks and reached the dock about noon time here. She was unloaded, recoaled, stocked and then reloaded with freight cars and passengers who waited from Saturday morning and to our surprise the ship made the return trip to Borden in one hour. One lady living in Souris said she was a passenger on her way to Montreal. On that trip Capt. Paquet carried her part of the way to shore.

Another incident remembered by Mr. O'Brien was this:
One day when the ship docked in Borden and we were coming up from the boiler rooms for dinner when we noticed a lone automobile on the flat car on the opposite side of the track as the shunting crew had removed the cars from the other side. There was a man, his wife and daughter, who came down from the passenger deck and when they saw their car on the other track started to walk across the car deck. In the dim light they failed to see one bunker grill was not in place and the girl stepped into the opening and fell into the coal bunker that was less than half full.

We turned back just to see what was wrong when the screeching woman said, "My daughter just fell through the ship." Men and lights were brought up and there she was, trying to scramble up the sliding coal in the bunker. She was soon rescued but her light coloured clothes were full of coal. She was a sight.

Walter O'Brien,
"Bristol Notes," *The Guardian*, September. 1983

Gracie Darling, circa 1905, wrecked on Panmure Island, circa 1926.
(Public Archives of Prince Edward Island)

1925 *Glyndon,* 99 ton, foundered in Northumberland Strait on September 24th. The next day, *Janet A,* 34 ton, stranded in North Bay, Stanhope. Both were out of Charlottetown. On October 26th, *Pacific,* 99 ton, out of Lunenburg, N.S., stranded in Summerside Harbour.

1926 *Ferguson,* 387 ton, of Halifax, foundered in Northumberland Strait on June 18th. On Sept 4th, *Malcolm Cann,* out of Yarmouth, 137 ton, also foundered in the Straight. *Mona,* out of Charlottetown, 87 ton, stranded in the Strait of Canso, N.S., on November 12th. *Fishborn,* 133 ton, out of Lunenburg, stranded at Cape Traverse on December 6th.

April 1926. Lovely fine morning, no wind, one could hear the rooster crowing, dogs barking, half mile up country — Souris train moaning for the crossings on her way to Charlottetown. The sun look as tho' it was not feelin' very good; the very fact you could hear the echo of the train-moaning as it came back from away off-shore, created an eerie feelin' that something weird is happening, weather wise.

A retired sea captain arrived from up country, we asked him what's his weather-forecast? He replied. Huge field of ice lying off shore on about 20 fathom, only visible from high land...coming towards the coast very fast, must be wicked on-shore tide, your lucky the season is not open. Later on that day, all fishermen were over on the high cape, east of the beach at Clear Spring...awe stricken, hypnotized and speechless as we watched the huge field of ice coming straight for the shore at unbelievable speed and not a breath of wind.

Our little beach and cove half mile long, was filling fast...the ice growled and thundered as it grounded on the rocks in the cove. And piled up two stories high against the high bank on each side of the cove...each berg telescoped under one in front.

Huge great rocks that have been there since creation were unceremoniously uprooted rolled over and then buried again or crushed in the terrible, unbelievable, appalling destruction of the coast.

Still the ice kept on coming after the cove was crammed full, on it came up over the dry sand away past high-water mark — still it continued, until everyone wondered where will it stop...then like a rumble away off in the distance, the real huge heavy bergs started rearing up in the air as they grounded in five fathoms...still the convulsions continued as the still heavier bergs continued the terrific pressure...

Sudden like you felt chilly, like the breath of a ghost on the back of your neck...sort of a bone-rattlin' shudder, you were blinkin' your eyes, at the change in the 'look of things' that occurred when you were so mesmerized...for instance, no one ever noticed 'Ol Sol' had gone to bed...the bone chilling atmosphere and most incredible, no wind.

Lorne S. Johnston, taken from his 35-year weather diary as a warning about building a bridge across Northumberland Strait. Even in the 1990s walls of ice, pushed up onto the cliff tops to form 25-foot walls, attracted much attention.

1927 *Edwards Falt*, 68 ton, of Charlottetown, stranded 4 miles west of St. Peter's canal, near River Bourgeoise, N.S., on August 24th. *Thelma*, 39.52 ton, of Annapolis Royal, N.S., stranded near the West River Bridge.

1928 The *White Bird* went aground on May 10, 1928, in the area north of the Boughton River (known to be treacherous and misleading to vessels). The 27.13 ton vessel had a cargo of fertilizer and bags of the water-soaked fertilizer were salvaged by residents in the area.

AN APPARITION

Many years ago a man from Little Pond went shooting. He built a blind out of seaweed, sticks, bushes. The ducks would come in so far and then fly out again before he could get a shot at them so he knew something was scaring them away. He decided to investigate and raised his head to peer over the blind. A huge snake-like head poked out from the weeds around the shore. He aimed and fired quickly at the monstrous head and killed it. However, the apparition began to thrash about in its last agony and the man realized how large the creature really was. He immediately took flight, dropped his gun, and raced to a nearby neighbours. The neighbours could hardly understand what had happened since he was almost incoherent with fright. They accompanied him back to find the carcass and discovered it to be fourteen feet long. They attached a wire to it and pulled it up. It was estimated to weigh close to 300 pounds. It was felt that this monster must have come from the sea.

Those Were The Days
A History of the North Side of
the Boughton River.

GAELIC THE KEY TO JACK MACPHEE

Not every shipwreck tale has an unhappy ending, as an article originally published in the *Family Herald* in 1928 proved.

Local storyteller Walter O'Brien proved the true expert on this tale, as usual! However, I can give the gist of the story.

There was a young man from Souris, who yearned to go to sea from the time he was a young boy. He wanted to sail the seven seas on one of the schooners that he saw in the port and dreamed of the wonders of the world. Jack was a determined young man, and he soon put dreams into action. Undoubtedly it was a happy young man who sailed from Souris as a crewman on a tall ship bound for China in search of a cargo of tea.

His family, however, became apprehensive when Jack failed to return. Months, then years, passed until eventually it was presumed he had been lost at sea.

The true fate of Jack MacPhee was not known for many years and then only came to light through the strangest of circumstance. It was 40 years hence when two other young men from St. Margaret's Village, near Souris, followed Jack's footsteps and also found themselves bound for the Orient.

After landing in Cathay, the two lads, along with other members of the crew, followed the tradition of all sailors coming to shore after long periods aboard ship, they headed for the taverns and other dubious entertainments available close to the docks. As is also often the case, they found themselves arrested for drunkenness and after spending the night in a jail cell were taken before the magistrate.

Now at that time, many citizens of the Island had the Gaelic as their mother tongue and would lapse into that language in times of stress. Such was the case with the two young Prince Edward Islanders. As the trial got underway they conversed not in Chinese or even English, but in their native Gaelic. In an unprecedented move, particularly in tradition-steeped China, the judge stopped the trial. At his command everyone was ordered from the room with the exception of the two young Islanders.

Imagine their consternation at the time. In a foreign land, where few spoke their own tongue, when everything was strange and most particularly the legal system. Now imagine their surprise when the judge spoke to them in Gaelic.

He told them that he was Jack MacPhee, the Jack MacPhee who had sailed from Souris some 40 years before. His schooner had wrecked on the coast of China and as best he knew he was the only survivor. The Chinese had found him clinging to a plank, alive but a stranger in his own body. He remembered nothing of his past.

Jack MacPhee literally began his life again in China. Kindly people took him in, cared for him and even taught him their language. An enterprising man, he was befriended by the judge, who taught him all he knew about their judiciary system. Jack became a respected member of the community and when the judge passed away Jack was appointed in his stead.

He remembered naught of his former home or of the circumstance of his arrival in China until the Gaelic spoken in his courtroom became the key that opened the door of his locked mind. By the time of revelation, Jack had a life in China which he did not wish to leave, including a wife and children. He felt he was too old to visit his land of birth, so he charged the two young men with taking the message back to the Island that he was well, and happy. He also asked that his name be added to the family headstone, below that of his parents, so that everyone would know what happened to Jack MacPhee

1929 *J.H. Ernest*, out of Charlottetown, 74.05 ton, foundered in Northumberland Strait on May 16. *Albert F. McWilliams*, 385 ton, out of Pictou, N.S., foundered, south 420°W from Sea Cow Head Light in Northumberland Strait on June 21st. *Whippet*, 6.12 ton, out of Ottawa, collided with "029" Lat 46°02'N, Long 62U°15'W, in Northumberland Strait on August 17th.

RUNNING THE RUM

The era of the rum-runner is one which holds much fascination, perhaps because the events occurred within the lifetime of some folks still with us today. There are many tales to tell, and to be heard.

Recently I was chatting with Floyd Serviss who owns New London Crafts and Antiques. I noticed he had some rum-running memorabilia and sweatshirts, and that led to talk of the era. Floyd has many tales to tell, one concerning a local resident, who as a boy used to take water out to the rum-running vessels. He would load up barrels of fresh water and row the three miles out to where the rum-runners considered themselves safe from the law.

He chuckled as he recounted the tale of the Government having the "limit" moved to 12 miles one day, which allowed the RCMP to capture the *Nellie J Banks.*

I must confess to knowing just enough about the rum-running era to be in danger of misrepresenting the facts, so I turn to more knowledgeable authority and urge you to do the same.

Here in Prince Edward Island we have one couple who have devoted much of their time to researching and documenting the history of rum-running and one particular boat, the *Nellie J.Banks.* Dr. Geoff and Dorothy Robinson live in Tyne Valley, one of the nicest villages on the Island and are the undisputed experts.

They have spent many hours tracking the history of various ships and crews. In fact, I would say they could almost pen another work about their own adventures! They have published two books on the topic, *It Came By The Boat Load* and the *Nellie J Banks.* Both are excellent reading if you want to learn more about rum-running. Dr. Robinson was the source of the information that follows; however, this only touches the surface of the story.

To set the scene let your mind go back some 60 years, to the 1920s. In the early 1900s Prince Edward Island was the first Canadian province to embrace prohibition throughout all of its counties. The province, according to powers-that-be, was dry. Of course we all know that decreeing something doesn't necessarily make it so. Prohibition did not result in a decrease in demand for liquor, but rather created problems of supply.

True there were no legal liquor stores. Temperance groups were strong and constantly waged war against those who liked to tipple the bottle. In the early 1900s it was customary for ships coming to Atlantic Canada from overseas to bring a number of kegs and cases of liquor with them. By 1923 vessels carrying only liquor started to appear off Canada's east coast.

The rum-running era had begun. Bootlegging gained a strong hold, and rum-running was almost common in certain circles as it provided employment for fishermen to transport the cargo. Those who entered what was in effect an illegal profession were looked upon with understanding by most. Times were hard; often the dangers of what they were doing were not offset by monetary gain. True a few made fortunes, but most eked out a living, especially if they were caught and had to pay fines, legal fees or had their boats and cargo impounded.

Some of those involved in rum-running were in search of an easy way to make money, or for the love of the challenge, of going against the odds, defying the law, and succeeding.

It was a smuggling operation pure and simple and needed the plotting, planning and skill of several individuals to be successful.

The contraband, or liquor, was brought back from vessels hovering off-shore outside the three-mile limit, according to Dr. Robinson. "A bootlegger would employ a co-operative fisherman to take off into the black of night to search for the mother ship anchored in a position that had been divulged to him."

"Fifty to 100 kegs would be transferred speedily and the fisherman would return to the wharf which was usually under surveillance by a family member who could signal if there was a problem. Once landed, Dr. Robinson says, "the next step would depend on the size of the purchase — a large number of kegs might be hidden in swamps or woods close by and guarded by a trusted employee until it could be relocated; otherwise it would be put into high-powered cars specially adapted to take kegs."

"The boot-leggers would head to Charlottetown or Summerside past the homes of Islanders who would hear the vehicles and know what had happened down at the shore."

"It was part of the rural life of P.E.I., tolerated for the most part with smiles over breakfast and educated guesses as to whom might have been involved."

The Robinson's stress that as this was a province that was supposed to be in favour of temperance, "It's surprising how much smuggling there was between the years 1923 and 1942."

> *It was said that the country was full of Prohibitionists until they went to the woods! In the early days it was mostly kegs of rum that made their way ashore, but later there was alcohol in 2 1/2 gallon cans that provided a ready base for crafty boot-leggers to convert into less potent liquids by the additions of water and powerful essences.*
>
> *Most of the rum was brought from Georgetown at the mouth of the Memerara River in British Guiana. The viscous Black Diamond variety was the favorite Maritime drink.*
>
> *Although all three provinces were soon heavily involved in the trade, once Canadian Rum-Row got under way in 1923, it is notable that the first three schooners that made initial voyages to Georgetown to bring up entire loads of rum to be peddled off the coast were all two-masted schooners closely associated with P.E.I.*

The Robinson's were able to confirm this when they visited Guyana, formerly British Guiana.

"They found that custom records of the port were no longer in existence after several fires, but they were able to examine newspapers in the archives to find that these three vessels, and three only, were collecting their cargoes in the summer of 1923."

Nellie J. Banks

Most infamous of all the rum-running vessels, at least as far as the Robinson's and P.E.I. are concerned, was the *Nellie J. Banks.* She has such a fascinating history that the Robinsons have written a whole book about her.

The *Nellie J. Banks* was the last fulltime rum-running schooner to be seized off the east coast of Canada. She was captured off Naufrage on August 9, 1938, by the RCMP vessel *Ulna*, and the three crew members were deported to Newfoundland, described as "natives of the Ancient Colony."

Capt. Israel Lillington, however, was imprisoned initially in Charlottetown and later in Georgetown while he awaited the preliminary hearing in which the magistrate sent him to the sitting of the King's County Supreme Court in the spring of 1939. Capt. Lillington spent the winter home on bail, returning to Georgetown where he was defended by J.J. Johnston, who was the outstanding criminal defence lawyer at that time.

Jury members were unable to agree on the decision that Capt. Lillington was guilty of contravening the Custom's Act and he was ordered to attend for another trial at the fall sitting. However, this was never followed up by the government, which felt that the chances of obtaining a conviction were very small.

Although Capt. Lillington was not found guilty, he had legal fees to pay and by virtue of the decision of the minister of Customs and Excise, the Nellie J. Banks was forfeit to the crown. She was subsequently bought by Capt. John Maguire of Borden, who named her after his daughter, Leona G. Maguire.

ULTIMATE FATE

The ultimate ends for many of the rum-running vessels proves as interesting as their smuggling careers. One ended up in Vancouver, was sold to Arctic entrepreneurs and sailed around Alaska to the roof of Canada. Another was purchased by Admiral Richard Byrd as a vessel for his Antarctic expedition. Others were purchased by the very governments that had been hunting them, and were refitted as preventive vessels, or revenue cutters. Yet others went to war in 1940 and were used by the Royal Canadian Navy. Many of the smugglers ended up fighting alongside the very men who had been hunting them down just a few years before.

Others, of course, had less romantic fates and ended up sinking, abandoned or legal trade.

1930 An explosion ripped through the *Amerob*, 40 ton, out of St. John's, Nfld, when she was off Miminegash on August 21st. On October 20th the *General Middleton*, 67 ton, out of Charlottetown, stranded near Wood Islands. *Freddie A. Higgins*, 78 ton, out of Charlottetown, stranded in Miramichi Bay on November 13th, and the *Shemogue* of Charlottetown was reported stranded on December 3rd, but no location was given.

1931 Three vessels registered in Charlottetown were lost this year: *Empress*, 612 ton, was destroyed by fire north of St. John Harbour, N.B., also the *Glooscap* out of St. John on June 15th; and the *Levis*, 23.89 ton, was stranded in Northumberland Strait on October 15th.

1932 The *Eva M. Prost*, 32.25 ton, out of Charlottetown, suffered an explosion on August 18th, near the lighthouse at Bedeque Bay in Summerside Harbour. *Wild Briar C.*, out of Charlottetown, stranded near Tignish on September 7th. *John C. Miles*, 32.14 ton, out of Sydney, N.S., stranded near Kings Head in Northumberland Strait on November 20th.

SEAPLANE SHATTERS CALM

Saturday, July 29, 1933, dawned a warm summer day, perfect for locals to flock to Crescent Beach in Victoria for a day at the shore. Little did those relaxing Islanders know that events which began in far off Italy would soon shatter their calm and generate much excitement in the seaside village.

It was the era that saw the birth of flight and the beginnings of it as a mode of travel. The Linbergs were "notables" after his transatlantic solo flight six years earlier; however, long distance air travel was in its infancy.

Senator Heath Macquarrie once wrote that it was Italy, then a major world power, that produced the most exciting innovation in the new aviation age.

"One of Mussolini's comrades in the famous 1922 Fascist March on Rome, General Italo Balbo, led a goodwill flight of 25 seaplanes from Orbetello in Northern Italy to Chicago, the site of the World's Fair."

Much publicity followed the flight which lost a plane in Amsterdam, and was feted in New York and Chicago. "Ottawa requested the armada to overfly our nation's capital. A P.E.I. youth was so anxious to see the Italian planes that he cycled to Shediac, one of the armada's Canadian stops. Needless to say my native village was not on the itinerary, nor did it request such an honor, but we had a visitation nevertheless.

"Fishermen and sailors naturally maintain an ever-alert seaward eye and it was not surprising that a mishap in the armada's Shediac to Newfoundland lap had occurred in our area. Charlie Miller and his son Reid set out in their fishing boat to tow in to port one of the craft which had come down in our harbor and while it is doubtful if his mandate included directing sea planes, he was early on deck," related Senator Macquarrie in the *Guardian-Patriot.*

Before noon the Italian plane was ashore where a crowd of Islanders had gathered. The first order of the day was to use one of the few phones available, and find someone who could converse in Italian. The crew were checked into the Orient Hotel (recently reopened!) and fed in the best Island tradition. The plane's broken water pump was repaired, probably too quickly for the likes of Islanders present, and the visitors soon took to the air again.

In 1933 we didn't see Benito Mussolini as the boastful braggart and sawdust Caesar which we later thought him to be," wrote Senator Macquarrie. Balbo became Governor of Libya and was killed in an airplane accident in 1940. In that year Italy went to war with prostrate France, and Canada and Italy became official enemies.

"But in 1933, even though Adolph Hitler was Chancellor of Germany, we were not apprehensive of the dictators of the right. Our security anxieties were expressed in other ways. Mussolini's right-hand man was seen in the heroic figure in our midst. But security demanded that Tim Buck, leader of Canada's miniscule Communist party, be incarcerated in Kingston Penitentiary."

1933 *Victor W.T.*, 98.78 ton, of Charlottetown, foundered one mile south of Blockhouse entrance to Charlottetown Harbour on November 10th. On December 19th, *Marguerite*, 74 ton, of Charlottetown, became a total loss off the southern coast of Barbados.

1934 *Eleanor R. Hammond*, 31.79 ton, of Charlottetown, stranded at House Harbour in the Magdalene Islands on April 30th. *Ronald M. Pearson*, 64 ton, of Charlottetown, sprung a leak near Miquelon on May 17th.

1935 *Chamecook*, 30 ton, of St. John, N.B., foundered 6 miles S.W. of St. Peter's Island Light on July 26th. On August 24, *A. Savoie*, of Chatham, N.B., 23 ton, foundered off Horse Head.

1936 Fire, was the cry heard from the *Enterprise*, 98 ton, out of Charlottetown, at the southern end of St. Peter's Channel on November 9th.

1937 *Eva Lloyd*, 12 ton, out of Charlottetown, was also ravaged by fire 10 miles off Pinette, on May 1st.

1938 Three lives were lost when the *Clarisse*, 55 ton, of Charlottetown, foundered one mile off Peggy's Cove in Nova Scotia on September 7th.

1939 *Florence G*, 52 ton, out of Charlottetown, foundered 4 miles south of Specers Island in the Bay of Fundy, on July 20th.

1941

WATERSPOUTS

When talking about strange phenomenon related to the waters surrounding Prince Edward Island, someone, sooner or later, will mention waterspouts, something best described as resembling a small tornado.

In early May 1941 a weird storm occurred in the East Point area. Now the East Point reef extends many miles out to sea. Neil Matheson described the reef in 1966.

"The average depth from the shore on out to the buoy would be approximately 50 feet. The average depth on the south side is 100 feet and rises almost perpendicular. The falling tide is the Northumberland Strait emptying into the Gulf of St. Lawrence pushed along at an average speed of four to five knots."

Neil went on to write that the turbulence created is really something to witness. It not only affected the water, but for some reason the winds, air currents and even temperatures above it.

"The vacuum thus created is of such magnitude that it pulls in air from surrounding areas with such force and speed that it gradually rotates from a corkscrew fashion into a rotating storm."

Lorne Johnston described one such storm in an "Ole Salt" column. "A weird storm occurred in the East Point area in the spring of 1941 during the early part of the month of May. One morning the wind was from the south on the south-side of the reef. On the north-side of the reef; the wind blew quite strong from the north. Wind velocity approximately 18-20 miles per hour, air temperature about mid-50s. All along the southern edge of the reef, where the turbulence was the worst, as far out to sea as visibility would permit, as many as four to six huge waterspouts could be counted. This phenomena lasted for the duration of the rising tide, which was flowing in the opposite direction to the south wind."

Waterspouts are certainly not a thing of the past, nor are they always associated with storms. In August 1993, a vacationing meteorologist had the thrill of a lifetime when he saw a waterspout from the beach at Tea Hill Park. The *Guardian* newspaper reported that Arnold Ashton of Toronto said he's travelled to Colorado and Texas hoping to see something like this, but never anything before the day we write about.

"I noticed billowing clouds around 12:50 p.m. Then this dark protuberance snaked down towards the water about a mile off-shore. It was pretty dramatic. All kinds of people were running around with cameras."

Mr. Ashton estimated the waterspout was about 4,000 feet high and several yards wide at the base. The weather forecaster for Environment Canada said the Island's weather conditions were ideal for the formation of waterspouts. Warm moist air rising from the water meeting with cooler air higher up. Indeed there were several reportings of other waterspouts during the hot humid spell.

The wind can often reach 50-60 mph at the water's surface. Waterspouts can obviously be dangerous, and powerful enough to capsize small boats.

WORLD WAR II — GERMANS CLOSER THAN YOU THINK!!

No one questions the involvement of Islanders in the battles of World War II. The province is well recognized for its high ratio of enlistment, both of men and women. As well, thousands of airmen from Britain received their training in the province.

Even with such strong links with the battles of war, most of us think of Canada as somehow isolated and safe from real danger. That simply was not the case. In fact it is downright scary to know just how close Prince Edward Island was to Nazi invaders.

"Ship sightings are not an unusual event on any river, however, in the year of 1938 a strange ship was sighted lying off Little Pond. This ship remained near the coast for two or three days and the sailors could be seen walking about on deck. The name of the ship was the *Bremner* and it was in fact a German Navy Training vessel probably engaged in coastal mapping procedures." — (*Those Were The Days.*)

On the west side of North Cape, close enough to shore that eyewitnesses were able to recount, a German U-Boat was sunk. Apparently the sub used to surface quite often as it laid in wait for ships passing by. One day in a joint operation between a plane and a patrol boat, the sub was caught on the surface. What was described as a direct hit on the stern caused the bow to rear up out of the water before the U-Boat plunged to the bottom. The year was probably 1941.

To check out this story one must talk to local fisherman who apparently know the location because their nets occasionally became entangled in the wreck which lies in about 14 fathoms of water. A munitions box has been recovered.

Another tale I've heard concerned a German who lived in hiding in the West Point area. The way it was told there was that a mysterious old woman would be seen at dusk, walking the beaches in the area. No one ever got near her or ever spoke to her, giving rise to stories of a ghost of spirit of some kind. Time passed, then one day some of the locals were called to lay her out for burial as the "woman" had passed away. When the attending citizens went to prepare the corpse in a decent manner, it was found to be a man in women's clothing. The assumption was made that it was a German, perhaps a spy, or a soldier escaped from one of the prison camps or a Navy man who had made it to shore and adopted the disguise to avoid detection.

The German presence was also felt in other areas of the Island. I've often heard that a German U-Boat used to lurk off the south eastern shore of the Island, but was never caught because it would lie in a deep canyon in the bottom of Northumberland Strait. Story is that local fishermen used to sell fresh produce, cigarettes and other items to the German sailors.

Lorne Johnston of Montague was truly an Island expert on tales of the past. Lorne was known as the Ole Salt, and wrote several books and a weekly newspaper column recounting tales of the past. I got to know Lorne when we both worked for the *Guardian.* He told me he remembered talking with an officer from *Fairmile*, a sub chaser that acted as an escort for convoys of freighters which travelled the Gulf of St. Lawrence during the war. These convoys used to sail from Sydney, Cape Breton, passing East Point then North Cape and Gaspé where they entered the St. Lawrence River. Presumably this route was taken to keep close to shore, and away from German submarines in the Gulf.

At least one ship, the *City of Charlottetown*, a Corvette, was torpedoed in the Gulf, according to fishermen in East Point who say they were told about it by a Mountie.

Fishermen reported sighting a sub about 10 miles-off shore all along the North Shore and up towards Cape Bear. According to Lorne, the officer from the *Fairmile* claimed the sub was never destroyed. The hole in the seabottom was presumed to be one visible on charts that lies between The Magdalenes and Prince Edward Island. It is said to be eight miles long, with an average width of two miles and is seven to nine hundred feet deep.

Could be the following incident is proof of the sub's presence.

Some miles due east of Murray Harbour lies a shoal known locally as Fisherman's Bank, named because it was a popular spot to net herring. These same nets often "caught" evidence of man and perhaps ships, wrecked in the area. Crockery, bottles and such did not cause quite the excitement that a German naval boot did when pulled up one day. Since no one could see the need for one German boot, it was tossed back, only to have the mate appear in the nets in another haul.

This area and that closer to shore around the mouth of Murray River has been the site of numerous wrecks, probably due to the deadly currents.

1941 Two interesting listings appeared in our research: On June 18, 1941, the *Charlottetown*, 3,385 ton, foundered off Port Mouton, N.S. In September, 1942, *Charlottetown* was recorded as being torpedoed and sunk by a submarine in the North Atlantic.

1943 *Senora*, 85 ton, out of Charlottetown, was stranded at Panmure Island on October 5th. The *Marilyn Michael* was lost out from the lighthouse.

1944 *Ernest 1.*, 18 ton, out of Bathurst, N.B., stranded in Northumberland Strait on June 13th. On September 15th, the *Mussolini*, 19 ton, out of Bathurst, had her sails ripped off by wind in the Alberton Harbour. On the 25th of September the *Nellie J. King*, 94 ton, of Charlottetown, foundered seven miles off L'Anse au Loup, Labrador. *Shag*, 37.5 ton, of St. John's, Nfld, was stranded on the Annandale Bar on October 9th. *H.K.P.*, out of Charlottetown, grounded at the Frand Entry Harbour, Magdalene Islands, on November 15th.

1945 An unregistered dump scow, the *Denton* overturned 1 1/2 miles S.W. of Port Borden on November 16th.

1946 Fire struck the *Nellie Dixon*, 60 ton, out of Charlottetown, on May 24th, near Flat Point, N.S. The *Francis Robie*, of Charlottetown, 28.33 ton, went missing with all her four crew in the Atlantic on November 11th.

HMCS *ASSINIBOINE*

Some time in the late 1940s a man was killed just off-shore of South Lake when trying to salvage a large brass propeller from HMCS *Assiniboine*. The ship had become stranded at the south end of South Lake Beach while being towed through Northumberland Strait sometime between 1945 and 1947.

Originally launched as HMCS *Kempenfelt* in 1931, she was sent to Canada and recommissioned as HMCS *Assiniboine* just after the outbreak of World War II. She had been sold for scrap after the war. The remains of the wreck are buried in the sand and occasionally a beachcomber will find a memento from the past.

FORERUNNER

There was an Island lad who joined the army during the war. He later transferred to the navy and sailed on the *Athabasca*.

One night his father heard his son come into the house, drop his kitbag onto the floor.

Then the father heard his son's footsteps going up to bed. So positive was the father that he went to investigate, thinking it odd that his son was home, when he should have been aboard ship. He found no signs of his son.

That very night the *Athabasca* was torpedoed and sent to the bottom of the Atlantic, The son was among those lost at sea. The father remained convinced that what he had heard was evidence of a forerunner.

During World War II many navigators and pilots for the British and Canadian airforces came to Prince Edward Island to learn skills needed for combat. Their presence had a profound effect on Island life, and they became fondly known as the Boys in Blue. These young airmen in training naturally had many tense moments during their Island training but perhaps none as dramatic as those rescued by Capt. Carl Burke.

On January 29th, 1943 The *Charlottetown Patriot* ran the following headlines on the front page:

V FOR VICTORY — The Charlottetown Patriot — V FOR VICTORY

Members A. B. C. — CHARLOTTETOWN, PRINCE EDWARD ISLAND, FRIDAY, JANUARY 29, 1943 — Single Copies Two Cents

RUSSIANS CAPTURE 33 TOWNS

Capt. Carl Burke Makes Thrilling Rescue Feat

THE RUSSIANS ADVANCE 45 MILES IN TWO DAYS

German Defences on Voronezh Front are Buckled as Russia's Triumphant Armies Advance within 75 miles of the Key German base at Kursk. 6,000 Prisoners are Taken.

ROOSEVELT IS BACK IN AMERICA

Good Progress in Big Steel Plant

Try to Explain Defeats in Russia

National Plan of Social Insurance

Is Included Among Measures Suggested as new Session of Commons Opens. System of National Health Insurance will be Studied.

Toronto Married Men 19-25 to be Called up

Sixteen Survivors

Four Airmen Are Taken From Ice Floe In The Gulf Of St. Lawrence

MANY SERBS ARE MADE HOSTAGES

Capt. Carl F. Burke Makes Five Perilous Landings on ice floe 20 miles off the North Shore of P. E. Island to Rescue Four R.A.F. Members and Valuable Instruments

NO FRENCH UNITY IN SIGHT YET

Island Native Is Promoted

The *Charlottetown Patriot*, January 29,1943 edition.

"CAPT. CARL BURKE MAKES THRILLING RESCUE FEAT;" "FOUR AIRMEN ARE TAKEN FROM ICE FLOE IN THE GULF OF ST. LAWRENCE."

"Capt. Carl F. Burke Makes Five Perilous Landings on ice floe 20 miles off the North Shore of P.E. Island to Rescue Four R.A.F. Members and Valuable Instruments."

The story of the thrilling rescue of four members of the Royal Air Force, marooned for almost 24 hours on an ice floe, 20 miles off Prince Edward Island when their Anson aircraft made a forced landing Wednesday afternoon, was unfolded in an interview this morning with Capt. Carl F. Burke of Maritime Central Airways. The airmen were uninjured in the landing and escaped not the worse for their harrowing experience.

At the risk of being caught in the same predicament as the unfortunate members of the light bomber, the youthful manager of the local airways company made a perilous landing in a one-passenger, Department of Transport plane on the ice floe about a quarter of a mile from the spot where the twin-engined Anson came down. One by one he then flew the men back to bases in Prince Edward Island yesterday in one of the most daring rescue feats ever performed in these parts.

Hopes of salvaging the bomber are slim as it is considered too risky. Today the ice is beginning to sag beneath it. Both the plane and crew drifted about 10 miles from their position 20 miles off the St. Peter's shore during Wednesday night.

Sleeping bags were dropped from the air to the marooned men late Wednesday and they were able to make use of their emergency rations during their stay on the ice.

Capt. Burke, modest by nature, was even more modest when questioned today about the heroic part he had played in saving the men. At the time the plight of the four airmen was learned, he was on a flight to the Magdalene Islands. On his two way radio equipment he was informed by the boys back at Maritime Central Airways office that the plane was down and four men marooned in the Gulf of St. Lawrence on a treacherous ice floe. The first indication of the trouble was radioed from the disabled ship by means of equipment on board. The men were in constant contact with the local base.

Capt. Burke altered his course on the way back to the Island and spotted the aircraft and crew below. He circled the spot several times sizing up the situation and sped back to Charlottetown with all haste. Another R.A.F. Anson was also surveying the situation while he was there.

The report brought back to the R.A.F. authorities by the manager of Maritime Central Airways was to the effect that only a small plane could possibly make a landing on the ice to rescue the men. As there were no small aircraft available here, a wire was sent to Moncton for help. The Department of Transport there sent a one-passenger Fleet here in answer to the appeal. However, there were no pilots with the proper knowledge or experience of ice conditions in that area to attempt the landing and Capt. Burke volunteered.

Yesterday morning he left the Charlottetown Airport and headed out over the Gulf. After circling several times near the stranded men, he spotted a landing strip and brought the plane down. It landed about one quarter of a mile from the Anson and the first crew member was taken aboard. This airman was then flown back to the Island and landed on St. Peter's Bay ice in the ski-equipped plane used by Capt. Burke in the rescue work. A second man was next flown to Charlottetown where the plane was re-fuelled about noon. Without loosing any time, Capt. Burke went back to the Gulf and picked up the third man and dropped him at St. Peter's. On the fourth flight he brought the last man back to Charlottetown.

His Fifth Flight

Making his fifth flight to the stranded ship, Capt. Burke salvaged radio equipment and flying instruments from the Anson and brought these back to Charlottetown.

The Manager of the Maritime Central Airways Company said it was a peculiar feeling to land in that desert of ice in the gulf. He wondered if he too might be forced to remain a prisoner on the floe with the airmen and did not fancy the prospect of having to walk perhaps about 40 miles, if even this were possible, to get back to land. However, fortunately for everyone, his skill in handling the aircraft made it possible to get all the men back safely.

1948 On April 10th, *Flying Fortress*, 13.3 ton, out of Lunenburg, N.S., went afire in Northumberland Strait. There was an explosion and fire aboard the 42-ton *Ernest G.*, out of Charlottetown, in North Sydney Harbour, N.S., on August 13th. *Hermada*, 94.37 ton, out of St. John's, Nfld., was stranded at the entrance to Georgetown on November 15th.

1949 A fire and explosion were reported on the *Millie B*, 20 ton, out of Charlottetown, on June 21, five miles E of Burnt Island, Atl. On December 5th, *Katherine G.* was destroyed by fire at Souris.

1950 *Gladiola*, 46 ton, registered at Charlottetown, grounded at Cape Auguette, N.S., on January 9th. On September 23rd, *Lantana*, 17 ton, registered at Bathurst, N.B., foundered and sank two miles southeast of the East Point buoy. *Lazy Mariner*, 39.74 ton, registered in Charlottetown, went on fire near Port Malcolm, N.S., on November 20th. On December 4th the *Mildred Burden* of St. John's, Nfld., 41.59 ton, went on fire and sank on the voyage home from Charlottetown.

1951 *Lorraine W.*, registered in Charlottetown, foundered 2 miles off Grey River on September 10th. On December 21st, *H.M. Nicolas*, 67 ton, registered in Charlottetown, grounded and sank at the entrance to Great Bras d'Or, N.S.

1952 February 28th the *Winnie Anne*, 19 ton, registered in Charlottetown, stranded three miles SE of Green Island, N.S. In December the *Six Four*, 41 ton, registered in Charlottetown, sprung a leak 30 miles SW from Channel Head, Cabot Strait.

1953 The *Elizabeth Alice*, 44.07 ton, registered in Charlottetown, caught fire June 26th at the north end of Canso Strait.

1955 *Ninety-One*, 44 ton, registered at Charlottetown, foundered off Newfoundland on April 14th. The *Jessie K*, 14 ton, also of Charlottetown, caught fire at Lat. 45° 50' N, Long. 61° 30'W. On December 14th, *Barbara W*, 22.14 ton, pending registration at Charlottetown, foundered at Howes Point, six miles SW of Souris.

1956 On December 17th, *Moose*, 27 ton, registered at St. John's, Nfld., went on fire six miles NE from Summerville.

1958 *Lidonna*, 17 ton, registered in Charlottetown, suffered an explosion and fire, Lat. 46° 40' N, Long. 61° 10" W, 12 miles west of Ingonish, N.S., on July 22nd.

1959 The *Prince Nova*, 297 ton, registered in Charlottetown, went on fire while moored at the pier in Pictou, N.S., on July 6th. The *Harry G.*, 34.10 ton, registered in Charlottetown, also went on fire in Pictou, at Purdy's Wharf on October 7th.

1962 *Caroland*, 65.65 ton, registered in Charlottetown, was in a collision with a minesweeper U.S. 292, approximately eight miles SE of the East Point Light on May 19th. On June 5th, *Earl John Miller* 33.70 ton, registered at Charlottetown, caught fire at the government wharf in Souris. *Irene Joan*, 19.67 ton, registered in Charlottetown, caught fire in the Montague River on August 22nd. September 29th, *Sailors Hope*, 6.36 ton, registered in Charlottetown, burned in Souris. *Gloria May*, 33.98 ton, of Charlottetown, lost a rudder and was stranded at Lat. 46° 24' 28"N, Long. 62° 03' 20" W, in Northumberland Strait on December 7th.

1965 On July 20th, *Donald And Eugene II*, 34.505 ton, of Charlottetown, went on fire at Lat. 45.51° 30' N, Long. 61°55 7' W.

1968 The *Donna Lynn*, 34.20 ton, of Charlottetown, foundered at Cape Smokey, N.S., on June 14th. On September 25th *North Bay*, 36.09 ton, registered in Charlottetown, caught fire at Cape George, N.S. A hurricane damaged several boats at Howards Cove on October 21st: *Darlene Dana*, *Peisa*, *Wendy C*, *Sandra G*, *Lee S*, *Mary Sophia*. All were registered in Charlottetown.

1969 *Prim Point*, of Charlottetown, was in a collision 10 miles from Wood Islands on September 13th.

IRVING WHALE CHECKED REGULARLY FOR LEAKS

In 1970, the *Irving Whale*, a barge loaded down with 4,200 tons of No. 6 fuel oil, went down some 50 km northeast of North Point, after water drainage through an open stern hatch.

Although the barge continues to leak fuel oil, it is not considered an environmental threat according to experts in Ottawa. Coast Guard ships check the site twice a year for oil slicks. Submersibles check the barge for visible leaks and so far say there is no evidence of observable impact on the environment. In 1977, 60 percent of the oil was estimated to be still on board. In 1985 a submersible check deemed the wreck in good condition.

The Coast Guard says that a salvage operation was never undertaken because of the risk of disaster. The *Irving Whale's* hatches and vents were sealed to contain the oil which was thickened by the cold water temperatures. The small amount of oil which does escape floats to the surface and breaks up within two kilometers of the wreck according to a report from Ottawa in May, 1989. It's now 1994 and studies continue. One must wonder when action will replace stalling tactics and the danger of a devastating spill will be eliminated. The Government is now taking steps to raise the the *Whale*.

Captain Ken Fraser's bluefin tuna put him into the world record books in 1979.
(*Guardian* photo)

1970 *Pauline,* 13 ton, registered in Charlottetown, foundered off East Point on August 17th.

1979

A BIG ONE THAT DIDN'T GET AWAY

A bluefin tuna caught by Island fisherman Captain Ken Fraser was officially a world record, weighing a whopping 1,496 pounds. The catch went in the International Marine Angler as "the all tackle and men's 130 pound line class world record." He hooked the big fish October 26th, off Auld's Cove, Cape Breton, and took just 45 minutes to land. A lobster and ground fisherman in season he had been fishing off North Lake without success and had been in contact with Nova Scotia fishermen. Because of licensing technicalities Island fishermen couldn't take their boats over so he joined Capt. Eric Sampson on board the *Lady and Misty,* with what he terms "my equipment and expertise."

The gigantic bluefin was ironically landed close where he had sighted his first tuna. During a nine-day span the *Lady and Misty* landed seven tuna. As to the catch itself, the North Lake fisherman said he, "couldn't believe it...couldn't imagine it...no one had ever seen a fish that big before."

From the time the fish was hooked no other person could touch the equipment until it was brought to shore. The scales on weigh-in must have been certified within the last six months; a sample of the line had to be provided; pictures of the weigh-in had to be taken in black and white along with a picture of the weigh-master, all of which had to be verified by a justice of the peace. The angler said even the scales were investigated by a N.S. Tourism official to be sure of the validity of the claim. All information had to then be sent to the International Game Fishing Association in Florida.

With the official recognition, honour poured in. The catch was written up as far afield as the *London Daily News* and included in a *Sports Illustrated* feature for which he received a handsome trophy. The fish was sold for $2 a pound.

1984

JOHN N. NEIL

There is another coal barge just east of Covehead Bay and this used to be one of the few wrecks visible on shore. In 1984 the skeletal wreck of the *John N. Neil* lay partially buried in sand about three miles east along the beach from the Blooming Point Road.

At that time it was estimated by locals that it had been there 100 years. Located on a relatively secluded fringe of beachfront, the grounded vessel looked like the bleached bones of a gigantic whale from a distance. As one walked closer it became apparent that the skeletal ribs were the timbers of the great wooden barge.

In 1984 at least 50 metres of the framework of the ship's hull bisected the beach fringe, with a protrusion from the bow sticking up out of the shallow water. The massive timbers for its keel are rotting somewhat, but seem incredibly well preserved considering the elements they are subjected to and the amount of water that will have broken over them. It is certainly the sand that has covered the ship's frame for so many decades which preserved it so well.

The wreck lies near Point DeRoche and whether it is now visible depends entirely on how the sands drift each year. Other visible wrecks have been seen near Savage Harbour and Tracadie Harbour.

LOBSTER LITTERING SHORELINE RECREATES HISTORY

The opening of the lobster season in late 1986 wrought havoc in the fisheries, particularly in Nova Scotia where stormy seas wrecked several boats and caused one drowning. Several rescues were effected, but Gery LeBlanc, a non-swimmer, could not be saved when his boat was swamped by a huge wave. Two others aboard clung to buoys until other fishermen arrived. Coast Guard spokesmen said it was an unbelievable day. Fishermen should not have ventured out with boats heavily laden with traps in the existing weather conditions, and to do so displayed a lack of common sense.

In Prince Edward Island evidence of this storm which caused such loss of life was to be with Islanders for several days. Thankfully, on the Island at least, it was not human life, but rather marine life that suffered.

Along the north shore of the Island from North Cape to Cove Head, bottom-dwelling marine life was tossed onto the shores in great numbers. Lobster, including egg bearing females, and very young lobster, plus a large number of rock crab also hit the shore.

Doug Rix from the Department of Fisheries in Charlottetown said that the lobsters were mostly dead when they hit the shore. Most had died from breakage between the body and tail section, although he said some had died from the severe cold experienced on the beach.

A team of biologists were brought in to work on the beaches. A square of about 2 meters every 500 yards was used to assess the amount of loss in the lobster population. It was felt the biologists would learn a great deal about the natural mortality of lobster in this process.

Though it seemed like an extensive loss to those who saw the lobster-covered beaches, Rix said there are probably events and diseases that have major effects on the lobster population that we never see. He said that in his 23 years with D.F.O. he had seen this sort of thing happen about five times without any adverse effect on the lobster catches the following season.

This event gave Islanders a little insight into the past, when such events seemed to happen much more often — probably because there were many more lobsters to be tossed ashore. In days gone by, it was written, lobster would be so thick a person could not walk on the shore after a storm. When the carcasses began to rot, it was an unfit place to be. Enterprising farmers could be seen the day after such a storm, filling wagons to take to their fields, for lobster is a great natural fertilizer. Even today rural people usually dump the carcasses from a lobster feed on the garden.

Tragedies remind us that the force of nature is as powerful today as it was years ago, and that man is just as vulnerable.

SKINNER'S POND MOSS FISHERMAN DROWNS

To those from away, it may seem strange to consider something done with a horse or tractor as part of the fishing industry. Strangely enough the harvest of Irish Moss does fall into this category and has long been an important source of income to many Island families. Many fishermen fish lobster in May and June, then gather moss at other times.

While the seaweed can be gathered by dragging a net or rake device behind a boat, this is not as efficient as the traditional method. After a storm as many able bodies as possible are to be found at the shore to gather up moss that has been ripped from the bottom by turbulent water and tossed onto shore. Rakes are dragged behind horses or tractors, the moss is loaded onto wagons and trucks and taken to a lawn, wharf or even the roadside where it is spread out to dry. The dry, clean moss is sold to companies who extract the carrageenin, a stabilizing ingredient used in making ice cream and other products.

This is one industry where the horse has remained king, it can get in places among the rocks and along the shore where a tractor cannot; it doesn't stall if the water gets a little high; and it doesn't do the environmental damage to the shore and the cliffs that a tractor can. Islanders and visitors alike love to see the big strong horses working in the surf, controlled by a rider who is usually a virile young man sitting bareback astride his working partner. It is not usual for accidents to occur, but considering the fact that the work is usually done in the surf that follows a storm, with footing that neither man nor beast can see and currents and tides to contend with, it is a dangerous business.

> *In late July of 1987, Albert Gerrard Ellsworth, 30, of St. Felix drowned while raking Irish Moss at Skinner's Pond around noon.*
>
> *Mr. Ellsworth was wearing an oilskin jacket and hip waders and had been riding a horse while raking moss. Sgt. Brian Robinson, officer in charge of the Alberton detachment, said the horse stumbled, losing its footing and fell into deep water. Sgt. Robinson was reported as saying Mr. Ellsworth stayed with the horse, but it began to drift further from shore. He said the surf was high at the time due to strong winds in the area. The horse also drowned and washed ashore.*
>
> *The police were aided in their efforts to locate the body by residents of the area, a search and rescue helicopter from CFB Summerside, and Red Cross water-safety personnel who had been conducting classes at the Day Camp being held at Skinners Pond Beach.*
>
> The *Guardian*, July 28, 1987

Conditions such as those on July 27th, when Mr. Ellsworth drowned, are usually good for Irish Moss fishermen who use horses in the surf to take the moss which has been broken off further out from shore and drifts in to the beach after high winds or a storm.

AROUND THE ISLAND THEY GO — MEETING THE CHALLENGE

Previous tales have told of the perils of the seas, of terror or lives lost. But it wouldn't be fair to leave the impression that the relationship of man and the waters surrounding Prince Edward Island are always such tumultuous and terrifying affairs.

There are good tales to tell. One of them from recent times involved John Barrett, who I've had some brief acquaintance with.

In the summer of 1987 John Barrett set out in a kayak to paddle his way around the Island. The trip had a combined reason. First and foremost, John loves to be on the water. He has ten years experience, kayaking in every province, except Saskatchewan, and in the U.S.A. The only months John didn't kayak were January and February, when it was hard to find open water.

Secondly, John wanted to raise money towards Cancer Research, prompted by the deaths of both his mother and father-in-law in a recent two-year period. The endorsement of the event by the Canadian Cancer Society turned the voyage into a major fund-raiser.

Even though the voyage began in July, all was not smooth paddling: John met two-metre waves and high winds; gales in fact sometimes forced him to shore.

Nancy Willis, a reporter for the Souris Bureau of the Guardian newspaper quoted John. "I'll never look at a map of P.E.I. in the same way again," he said, after his new intimate knowledge of every cove and inlet of the provincial coastline. "Now when I see the Island on paper or flying by air, I'll understand what astronauts who have been on the moon feel when they stay looking at it in the night sky."

John was not the first to paddle his way around the Island. Bill Reddin did it more than 50 years ago. Even though some people thought him a "damn fool" he says he just thought, "If I was foolish enough to start the trip, I might as well finish."

He began in 1934 and recounted that the trip was dangerous, especially where there was no beach, "just cliffs." Out in the high swells he was about six kilometers from shore and his canoe would be pitching about in waves as high as four metres. He had to break the voyage when winter set in, but completed circling the Island in 1935.

"I felt like a seagull out there, just going up and down. I didn't like that because I couldn't see where I was going."

Bill was without the support group that John had behind him, but he did have company. He was accompanied by his homely English bulldog, Bozo, and named his canoe Toto. Bill wrote a book *Canoe and I* some 30 years after his adventures which is still popular because of the wit and heart-warming reminisces expressed by the author.

DIVER LOST IN MURKY WATER

For those who make their living working in or on the water, not all danger is linked with boats. Consider the plight of an unidentified diver who got lost under the ice in the Boughton River near Montague.

During the winter of 1988, the diver was following the usual practice for harvesting mussels. A hole was cut through the ice, a rope attached to the diver and in he went. His job was to free the lines holding stockings of mussels in the water, so that they could be taken up through the hole for harvesting.

When the diver's "follow rope line" became untied under the ice he was left with no link to the surface, and no directional guide back to the hole which allowed him to leave the water. The rope line is connected to above-ground operations and allows the diver to find his way back to the surface through the murky waters. Imagine the feeling of following the bubbles upwards to be confronted with a barrier of ice as far as the eye could see, and knowing it stood between you and life-giving air.

Those on the surface quickly contacted officials for emergency assistance, but fortunately the diver managed to find his way back to the outlet and re-appeared before his air supply ran out.

1989

SEA SCOUTS ENDANGERED

In 1989 thousands of Boy Scouts came to Prince Edward Island to participate in the Canadian Boy Scout Jamboree held at Fort Amherst. They elected many methods of travel, but none quite as adventurous as a group of Halifax-area sea scouts who decided to sail.

Sea Scout I, a 10-metre whaler, was travelling from Skinners Cove, N.S., to Charlottetown when it ran into trouble near Point Prim, just south of the city's harbour. The whaler hit two successive two-metre waves, which tipped the boat's mast into the water and then caused it to overturn.

The five sea scouts and two adult leaders on the boat were in the very cold water for some seconds, until they were able to swim back to the upside down whaler. They clung to the bottom of the boat until rescued by other boats who were travelling in a flotilla of two other whalers, a 10-metre and a six metre-sailing boat.

After the accident, and rescue, the other boats removed their sails and everyone travelled by engine through the choppy seas and into safe harbour. It took six passes by other boats to rescue the crew and equipment from the boat which was then left adrift.

The Canadian Coast Guard escorted the convoy to safety and later commended the sea scouts and leaders for their extensive training and experience. "They were ready for it, and it showed."

1989

LORNE MISENER REMEMBERED

During one brief stint in my career, I worked at Stanhope Beach Lodge in a position which often meant staying overnight as my duties started at the crack of dawn. It was there that I got to know a charming chap by the name of Lorne E. Misener, a local who fished out of Covehead Harbour. Lorne, or "Duke" as he was known to family, used to supply the Lodge with fish, and would also come to pick up his wife from work, or just to hang around with the gang.

Lorne often told me he couldn't understand why enthusiasts didn't dive off the north shore of P.E.I. more than they do. Historical data tell us of many, many shipwrecks. Fishermen like Lorne knew the locations of many wrecks, usually because they had some effect on their fishing. Nets catch in wrecks, they can effect the flow of water, and they can become great habitats for marine life.

Lorne used to tell me of the presence of a coal barge in just 50 feet of water, just northeast of Covehead Harbour.

"When you get certain lobsters in your traps you know you're on it, they're right black," he used to grin. The black was coal dust!

Members of the Misener clan also found proof positive of wrecks of the past in the form of an ancient anchor, hauled up in their nets in 1986. It was estimated to be 200 years old.

Lorne Everett Misener, 34, of Union Road was killed July 20, 1989, when he got caught in nets being hauled aboard his own boat. He had gone fishing alone off the north coast of the Island early in the morning. About three hours later, around 9 a.m., nearby fishermen noticed his boat drifting.

When they climbed aboard, they found Lorne wrapped around a hydraulic spool which pulled the heavy nets from the sea. When his foot became entangled in the net he was unable to reach the control that would have stopped the engine. Lorne, and the net were wrapped around the large spool and he was literally beaten to death. If Lorne had not been at sea alone, he would still be with us today. Those of us who knew him, even slightly as I did, wish desperately that he had not been alone that day.

Lorne had a rich heritage of the sea. As a young boy he would hang around at the harbour, fishing every time he could. He fished with his father for a time, but when he passed away, Lorne began going out alone. He once told me some thought fishing "a hard way to go" but that was the life for him.

1989

DRAMATIC RESCUE OF GENTLE GIANTS OF THE DEEP

The relationship between man and the mighty whale has formed strong bonds in recent years. A human empathy with this warm-blooded mammal who is a closer relative to us than any other sea dweller is only natural. Thus, when six sperm whales became trapped between sand bars at Covehead on the Island's north shore at the beginning of October 1989, a rescue effort was mounted. Their success gained the fishermen, divers and officials international recognition.

With a great deal of co-operation and a "let's just go out here and get this job done" attitude, the whales were taken off the beach and four of the six are thought to have survived.

It was one of the most emotional experiences that many of those present will ever have. Feelings ranged from rage of helplessness, tension of hope, despair of failure and finally heart-swelling pride in the men who pulled off what many said was impossible.

The events began when the whales, beached on sandbars about 549 metres(600 yards)off shore, were first spotted early Sunday morning, October 1st 1989, and reported to Fisheries and Oceans Canada by the RCMP. Word soon spread even though the only media operating from the Island that day were local radio stations.

So great was public interest that park wardens stopped cars heading for the disaster area, turning back the majority of traffic. The Covehead Bridge was out for repairs and parking at the site limited. Park officials were concerned about excessive numbers of people damaging the ecostructure of the dunes, injuring themselves on the bridge, and perhaps hampering the rescue operation. Even so, thousands of people parked their vehicles and walked up to five kilometres to reach the whales. Official estimates are that up to 10,000 people viewed the whales that day.

As I arrived, more than a dozen people came up over the dune, dejectedly walking away. Some were wiping tears from their eyes. My heart dropped. What horrible event would have caused people to cry on this sunny fall afternoon. Should I stop here and avoid the sadness that awaited over the ridge of sand?

"The rope broke," sniffed one woman in response to my worried query. Thanking God that a more gory sight wasn't waiting, I crested the dune. My heart seemed to fly into my throat. Five whales were thrashing just yards from shore, seeming oblivious to divers in their midst. A sixth whale was quiet, but I could discern some movement (now I realize that was probably caused by the water action). My first reaction was pleasure, they were still alive; and fighting. There was hope.

Concern was evident as hundreds of Islanders looked on in silence as rescue attempts were made. Most could only take the observer role. Too many people in the water would have hampered the efforts of the few who took on the task and further frightened the thrashing whales. Many of us kept the vigil all day and into darkness, feeling that our very presence would somehow influence the outcome of the drama taking place. Personally there was a sense of shame that I stayed on shore watching others do what I wished I could. Even though realistically I knew that I was neither equipped nor physically fit enough to do any good if I did enter the water, I felt deep regret at my own inaction.

These photographs of the rescue of beached whales at Stanhope in 1989 were taken by the author, Julie Watson, from the shore. They were reprinted in numerous publications at the time.

Fishermen and fisheries officers worked together to develop a plan of action. Federal fisheries officers, coordinating efforts on shore, called in divers John Barwise and David Gormley of Underwater Services. They were joined by John MacLeod, Roger Jones, Dave Cosh and Neil McNair. Basically the plan was simple. A rope would be placed around each whale and it would be towed out to deeper water.

Simply said, but not simply done when dealing with thrashing mammals whose sheer mass was estimated at between 40 and 60 tonnes. Time and tide proved to be major obstacles. The tide was low during most of the operation and those involved feared that if effort to free the whales were not carried out as quickly as possible the results would be devastating.

The first effort to tow the whales failed when tow ropes snapped and several frustrating hours of waiting followed while a heavy rope was found and delivered. Divers seldom left the whales alone. As the tide turned and more water flowed in there was some hope that they would be able to help the whales turn and somehow escape. It was a futile wish.

As evening approached the rope arrived, the tide was in and activity escalated.

Mr. Barwise said the amount of time required to secure the whales varied from whale to whale, though in most cases it was about ten minutes. Divers in wet suits waded out in water up to their shoulders, approached the whales from the rear, secured the ropes to their tails and then swam the line to boats which dragged the whales to open water.

"If we were quiet around them, and didn't bother them too much, they let up put the ropes around them. Once they felt the rope go tight though they started to thrash, and when the boats started up, all hell broke loose. They went absolutely crazy."

None of the divers were injured, but the potential for injury was very real, especially as the cold water temperature and many hours working with the whales caused severe fatigue.

"Nobody got hit by a tail or anything," said Barwise. "A good thing. If that didn't kill you it would certainly have done a lot of damage. We did get bounced around a bit though, from the water."

None of the divers said they were apprehensive about being involved in the rescue effort.

"I was more excited than anything I think. It was a great experience. I really enjoyed it although we felt bad for the whales. They were pretty helpless."

David Cosh described the whales, "All I can tell you is they've got a great big mouth full of teeth," he grinned. "We can climb on them and pass the rope underneath. They know we are there and are pretty docile. You can hear them clicking." He said the main danger was from the tails which were described as "hard, like rubber."

Other divers mentioned the noises the trapped whales made, saying it sounded like crackling. Their greatest fear was that the huge mammals would just wear out and die.

While the efforts of the divers were the most visible, it was perhaps the fishermen who were the real heros of the hour because of their sheer determination to rescue the whales.

John Myers, Captain of the *Cape Cove II* credited Freddy Morrison, Captain of the *Covehead Rover,* with doing the majority of the hauling. Richard Roberts and Linus Misner captained the other two boats involved in the hauling.

Once the line was attached to the whale and passed to the boat, each whale was towed out about 100 metres and then circled, to discourage it from returning to the beach. The weight and bulk of the whales required two boats pulling together to move them. The roaring motors, straining, could be heard over the surf.

While he's seen other whales beached, Mr. Myers said he had never seen anything quite the same.

"I've never seen anything like that before. I wasn't scared but it was a little anxious. You didn't know how far to take your boat in, it was hard to see the bottom at times and sonar can't be relied on all the time at that depth."

There was also the danger of the rope snapping, and even of the strain proving too much for the boat or its motor.

Perseverance paid off, however, and all the whales were towed off that evening. One washed ashore at Covehead that night. Rescuers were quite sure it was dead when they towed it off, but fears of the others coming back to it and getting stranded again, mixed with hopes that it would revive, were enough to put the effort into pulling it into deep water. A second corpse washed ashore at Hamilton, on Malpeque Bay on October 5th. Both carcasses were buried, but the skeletons will be unearthed in a few years, one bound for the New Brunswick Museum in Saint John and the other to Ripley's Believe It or Not Museums.

While those in and on the water received most of the credit for the rescue, it was a fully co-operative effort, also involving staff from the Canadian Coast Guard, Parks Canada, Fisheries and Oceans, and many volunteers.

It is not known what caused the whales to become trapped between the two sandbars, but a Federal Fisheries spokesman theorized that one possibility is that the sound of a jackhammer working on the Covehead Bridge attracted them.

Whatever the cause, the incident left a lot of people feeling good about the efforts that had been made to rescue these gentle giants from the deep. It was a quiet kind of feeling good that goes to the heart.

Lorne Misner said it best during a television interview. "There was no need of them dying there. No need."

1989

KILLER STORM CLAIMS LIVES

In early December 1989, a terrible storm raged in the Gulf of St. Lawrence. Two ships were lost even though rescuers may have come within sight of some of the 39 foreign seamen missing after the two ships capsized. By nightfall on December 8th, no trace was found of any of the 23 crewmen of the 127-metre *Capitaine Torres* bound for Taiwan from Montreal, or 16 people aboard the 91-metre *Johanna B* bound for eastern seaboard ports in the U.S.

During the same storm a giant salt barge, the 14,000-ton *Captain Edward V. Smith* the size of two football fields, with 190,000 litres of diesel fuel aboard, was secured with a tow line to prevent it from crashing into Cape Breton's rocky coastline. The vessel had been steadily heading closer to shore west of Cheticamp, N.S. The tug *Arctic Nanook* was towing the barge about 70 kilometers to an anchorage near Souris. The barge broke free of its tow line during storm conditions off the Gaspé Peninsula. She was eventually landed in Georgetown for repairs. The incident sparked concerns about the environmental damage which would have resulted had she broken up and lost the fuel.

1990 March 2nd – ICE TRAPS 30 VESSELS IN GULF

An early winter, unusually low temperatures and easterly winds combined to make ice conditions the worst in 10 years according to the *Evening Patriot.*

"It's so bad, even the icebreakers are having trouble." The speaker was one Capt. Bert London. He and his crew of 15 aboard their oil tanker, the *Imperial Bedford,* were one of 30 ships stuck in the ice. The skipper wasn't too concerned. A Newfoundlander with 27 years experience in the Gulf said he'd take the metre-thick ice over an Atlantic gale any date.

"We're not getting anywhere, but it's nice and comfortable. We've got lots to eat, lots of television — all the conveniences really." At the best of times, the 14,000-tonne *Imperial Bedford* was moving a ship's length at a time in a procedure London calls "back and fill — we go ahead so far, back 'er up and ram it again."

1990

MODERN RESCUE BY 413 SQUADRON

May of 1990 brought forth a recurrence of storm-tossed seas and a dramatic rescue by 413 Squadron based at CFB Summerside. Their mission began at 4 pm, May 11th as a Labrador helicopter, en route from Magdalene Islands(where it had refuelled)to Gander, Newfoundland, was contacted by the Rescue Coordination Centre in Halifax.

They were told a 130-foot private ferry, the *Tessa Kathleen,* was in distress ten miles off the tip of Anticosti Island. It was sailing from Windsor, Ont., to Bombay, Nfld.

Captain Michael Mayhew, commander of the mission, later explained that the ferry's anchor had broken and they had to cut it off, and then had only limited steering. By that time the helicopter was just 40 miles from Stephenville, Nfld., however they turned around and arrived about an hour later to find the ferry in dire straits.

Winds were gusting up to 70 miles an hour, sea-swells were 30–35 feet. The little vessel was being pounded, severely and was "all over the place."

"By times we could see two-thirds of the underside of the boat," Captain Mayhew was quoted as saying in the local newspaper, the *Journal Pioneer*. "We were afraid it was going to capsize."

Under these conditions the perilous rescue began. Two search-and rescue-technicians, M-Cpl. Jim Brown and M-Cpl. John Tremblay, were lowered by cable onto the ship. Captain Mayhew, Capt. Chuck Grenkow, first officer and M-Cpl. Kevin Gignac, flight engineer, conducted the operations aboard the helicopter. The operation involved one of the technicians staying on the vessel, and the other being harnessed to one survivor at a time, hoisted off the ship and into the hovering helicopter.

But then things started to go wrong.

One of the eleven survivors on the ferry was a woman, who was to be the first hoisted to safety. The harness was secured and she and the technicians were ready for the lift.

"The cable got stuck, or birdnested," explained Captain Mayhew. "The boat pitched a couple of times and that was it — the cable had to be cut. The woman was on deck with the two technicians and 100 feet of cable, and they weren't looking very happy."

A second helicopter was summoned, but great concern was felt about the time it would take to arrive and the safety of the stranded sailors and technicians. The decision was made to attempt the rescue with a back-up hoist located on the centre hatch of the helicopter, as opposed to the primary equipment which operated from the side of the aircraft. The back-up hoist is slower and less efficient, but under the circumstances, they felt they had no choice but to use it.

"We started taking them off and after the first one, knew it was going to go alright," said the Captain.

It was not an easy rescue. The boat was pitching around so erratically that it was hard to predict which way it was going. At one point Capt. Mayhew said it came within three or four feet of the helicopter.

The actual hoisting operation took about 75 minutes. After being on the scene for more than two hours, the helicopter headed for Gaspé. Tension mounted as the fuel gauge dropped lower and lower. Just minutes before the supply would have been exhausted they were able to set down.

"It was nice to see the ground," Capt. Mayhew commented, "We landed with eight or nine minutes of fuel left, but our gas gauges also have a six-minute fuel error, so you never know!"

The Labrador was shadowed by two support aircraft during the rescue, an Aurora from Greenwood, N.S., during the first part, and then a Buffalo, also from Summerside. The Buffalo's crew had calculated there would be enough fuel to make Gaspé.

SAME WEEK — MORE HAVOC

That was not the only drama of the week, although it was the most high-tech and dramatic.

A fishing boat went aground on a sandbar at the entrance to Skinner's Pond harbour. The boat, along with all the electronic equipment aboard was destroyed. Another fisherman, Myles Ellsworth, had been stuck on the sand bar when Gerard Ellsworth attempted to pull him off. He then got trapped on the bar himself.

While he was stuck there, his vessel turned on its side and filled with water. In addition to writing off his boat and equipment, Ellsworth lost his catch of herring.

Fortunately all aboard were rescued and Mr. Ellsworth was able to continue fishing using his brother's boat. Locals blamed drifting sand for the accident and called for more dredging.

1991 March — Six Tignish men experienced an adventure when they snowmobiled around the Island, mostly on the shore ice, covering 462 miles in all. They averaged speeds of 40 to 45 miles per hour and took three days. They had originally planned to head for the Magdalene Islands, but it was clear the Gulf ice wouldn't hold a party of snowmobilers, so they changed the route of their fund-raising event.

1991 March 30th — *The Guardian* reported northsiders at Campbell's Cove were treated to a weird experience Wednesday past, when they clearly saw what appeared to be the lights of the Iles de la Madelines over 70 miles across the water — a sight that should be physically impossible. Be that as it may, several households confirmed the sightings, which included dotted lights scattered randomly, a string of stationary lights, and others moving. Also clearly showing was the beam of what they believe to be the eastern-most lighthouse flashing its regular signals. Weatherman Alva Cleary, said it is not normally possible to see beyond 15-20 miles because of the earth's curvature. Even with the boost of 50-foot northside cliffs, the Iles de la Madelines still lie too low in the water to be seen. But in nature anything is possible. Mr. Cleary said there was a swatch of open water around the Islands with heavy ice packs just beyond, and given the unusually bright clear conditions, it could be possible people were seeing a reflected image. He said in the north, mirages or images of things hundreds of miles away have been reported during uncertain conditions. Flora Campbell, who lived on the northside all of her life, said she has seen this phenomenon only twice before.

1991 June 15th — Fishermen were waiting to assess damage caused by a storm that lasted several days. The storm also took its toll elsewhere as well, when storm-driven tides destroyed 20 nests of the endangered Piping Plover in P.E.I. National Park. Officials reported the highest tide seen for that time of year which also flooded breeding grounds in tidal marshes.

Meanwhile, officers and crew aboard the CCGS *Tupper* were caught by surprise when lightening struck the water just off the port side, shattering a window in one of the ship's cabins. The sea had been fairly calm but immediately the weather turned very ugly.

1991

OPERATION LANCER

Shortly after midnight on an isolated beach near Clear Spring, RCMP on the ground surrounded ten men who had unloaded 20,000 pounds of marijuana from a yacht offshore. A helicopter swooped down and fixed a powerful spotlight on the scene. "Operation Lancer" netted $20 million worth of drugs, making it the biggest drug bust in P.E.I. history. The *Nic Nac*, towed into Charlottetown port under arrest on August 27th, 1991, to be searched by RCMP, fits the description of boats typically used by drug traffickers. It was small(only 12 metres long), low-profile, single-masted, and made of wood and fiberglass painted dark blue. These characteristics increase the traffickers chances of evading detection by radar or surveillance across the water. Kind of puts one in mind of the Rum Runners way of thinking.

Journal Pioneer — August 28th, 1991

1993

Sub-zero temperatures wreaked havoc on both land and sea during February, 1993. While homeowners wrestled with frozen locks and broken water pipes, sea captains faced more serious consequences that could threaten the safety of their ships and crew.

> *Although all appears well now with the Latvian freighter **Zenta Ozola**, as it lies dockside in Souris taking on potatoes, Capt Petr Thachenko would only know for sure when got back up to full steam in open water. As the ballasted ship made its way into port last week, the thermometer dropped to -30 Celsius, and ice surrounding Prince Edward Island made manoeuvering impossible.*
>
> *The Canadian Coast Guard ice-breaker **Earl Grey** picked up the **Zenta Ozola** and its companion ship the **Akademiks Hohlovs** somewhere off Cape St. Lawrence, Cape Breton, but the ice was so thick that by nightfall it still wasn't able to get them moving. The larger icebreaker, **Sir William Alexander**, was called in and succeeded in leading them free of the main floe, then left for another ship in trouble and the **Earl Grey** wouldn't take Capt. Thachenko's vessel on to Souris that night. As a result, he was forced to sit for eight hours as the ice moved in around him. He said it was especially bad because they were sailing with empty holds and only a seawater ballast.*
>
> *Under those conditions, the ship is light and rides high in the water, leaving it extremely vulnerable. The Captain was used to Ice Service Riga in the Baltic Sea, where icebreakers never stop. The Captain would not know if damage was done to the vessel until they left to head for Portugal and Turkey with their load of potatoes.*
>
> Nancy Willis reporting in the *Guardian*

AND FINALLY.....CONCERN

In these days when the whole world is more conscious of preserving the environment and protecting the creatures that share the earth, Prince Edward Islanders find themselves in a position to be envied. The over-industrialization and over-population that have done severe damage to less fortunate places are not a factor here.

These days we hear much about saving our forests and cleaning up land and air pollution. The voice to preserve the margins of the sea is faintly heard from time to time, but is not strong enough yet to be considered part of the environmental chorus.

Robert Cowen recently wrote, "Unwise development and excessive population growth press hard on the world's coastlines and offshore waters. They foster destruction of important habitats and tarnish the livability of coastal regions."

Here in P.E.I. we are doubly blessed. Concerned citizens fight to protect our shore, and slow growth has done minimal damage. Problems such as processing plant and agricultural-run off, and damaging development must continue to be addressed, however, and all citizens should throw their support behind those who take the front line stances. In our beautiful province it is easy to be lulled into complacency. That we cannot do.

A reminder of our good fortune is to be found in the flourishing marine mammals and bird life of our coast. For those interested in commerce, these should be counted as the asset they are. Already we have seal and bird-watching boat tours. Some enthusiasts now hire fishing boats to photograph wildlife, rather than hook it. Seals and cormorants should not be considered a competitor by fishermen, but rather an alternate source of income.

The osprey, or fish-hawk, is protected by the P.E.I. Fish and Game Protection Act with a maximum fine of $1,000 and a minimum fine of $200 or up to six months in jail; all articles seized are forfeited to the Crown. Unfortunately, there is no direct legislation to protect their habitat.

There are approximately 50 known osprey nests on the Island, seventy percent of them in Prince County. High winds destroy nests and blow down nesting snags. In 1975 a nest blew down at Belle River. An artificial nesting structure was built and two young osprey were successfully reared by the adults. Subsequently, two wagon wheels were placed in nearby trees and the adult birds returned to raise young on one of these wheels for the following five years. Other artificial nesting platforms have been built with some success.

As a result of the efforts of conservation officers and other bird lovers, and the banning of the DDT chemical, the osprey are making a comeback and can be considered as encouragement for other projects.

The eagle, too, is a known presence on the Island, and protected under the same law. We've had the opportunity of observing a nesting

Osprey, such as this, cormorants nesting, even eagles can be spotted by the observant. The best place to see wildlife today is from a seal-watching tour, "Up East". (P.E.I. National Park photo)

eagle this year, through binoculars, and urge everyone to protect the environment used by these great birds.

Perhaps the most widely published preservation efforts taking place on the Island are those of the P.E.I. National Park to protect the nesting environs of the endangered Piping Plover. Birdwatchers and naturalists can learn much through programs offered by the parks and environmental organizations. A walk along the shore can reveal many shore birds, as well as give a feel for the sea like that experienced by mariners past and present.

Just feet away is the environment of marine mammals. Our Island is not well publicized for the presence of seals, whales, porpoise and such because they are not highly visible. They are there however. In 1985, when one driver watched their antics instead of the traffic ahead, he tied up traffic on the Hillsborough Bridge, causing an accident. A year earlier six porpoises were stranded at Vernon River when the tide went out. Some onlookers, seeing the dorsel fins sticking out of the water, thought that the harbour was being invaded by sharks while others though they were whales.

Sharks are often caught by fishermen, and in 1982 a 9-meter, grey-basking shark travelled up the Hillsborough River as far as Mt. Stewart. The shark was well inland and swimming around right up against the causeway. It had fins up to two meters and "was quite a sight," according to fisheries officer Florian Bryant. A local fisherman found the shark when he was starting his oyster operations in the morning.

It is uncommon to see a shark that far inland, but it, like the porpoise, seals and whales that come close to shore, was likely following a school of fish.

I particularly remember that incident as I was working at the newspaper at the time and spent some happy hours careening around the countryside with our son John, trying to catch up to it for a photograph. We also spent hours hanging over the edges of wharfs in Charlottetown one cold winter's day, angling for a good shot of a whale that came into the harbour.

Blue whales are enjoying the hunting hiatus in the Gulf of St. Lawrence. A 23-metre Blue beached in Norway, near Tignish, on November 12th, 1987. The 80-ton whale died and was buried in a pit near where it beached. Residents were not all pleased to see the burial take place as it had created a mini-tourist boom in the area. A sperm whale came ashore off Nail Pond December 16th, 1988. Blues and other whales can sometimes be spotted from boats quite close to shore.

We just have to hope they don't all go the way of the beautiful Beluga which are being destroyed by toxins and pollution in waters off Quebec shores.

Seal herds are reasonably common and can be seen by taking a tour from Murray River or Murray Harbour, or hiring someone familiar with the waters to take you to Governors Island, off Tea Hill. Seals are also seen from North River Causeway in the winter. It always gives me a lift to spot one watching morning traffic headed to the city.

In 1993, tourists were thrilled to see a pod of hundreds of whales just five minutes east of Souris Harbour. Captains George and Bev Roach, operators of Souris Light Cruises, said they had never seen anything like it. For three quarters of an hour one evening in late July their 15-metre fishing-tour boat cruised among a group of Pilot whales that lolled and jumped around it as far as the eye could see. Right to the horizon they could see them leaping from the water.

"There were literally hundreds of them," said Mrs. Roach in a *Guardian* report. The adults appeared to be in the 20-to 30-foot range, and there were babies and juveniles of every size. They were swimming in a relaxed manner, lolling in the sun and diving. Often four or five swam so close together they were touching, even coming out of the water in unison. As the boat drifted with them, its engine idling, the huge mammals would swim contentedly beside, then slowly pull ahead. When they outdistanced him, Mr. Roach would get his engine going and catch up with them again. He said they didn't seem to be the least bit upset that we were there, and just continued swimming round us with their babies. The fish were black with a large dorsal fin, and long pectoral fins that looked almost like arms.

Just days after this sighting, we were coming home on the Wood Islands ferry and saw, what we believe was probably members of the same pod. We were not as close, so cannot be sure whether they were whale or dolphin — but even so it was a thrilling sight for us and the tourists we pointed them out to.

We must work to preserve these wonders, and renew the natural marine life of our waters. And we cannot be complacent. The *Irving Whale* still leaks its oil. Pollution on a small scale over a number of years, is not really an acceptable alternative to remedying the problem! Islanders are being trained for cleaning up spills, and environmentalists must still work diligently against too much opposition to protect nature. We have a long way to go!

A BOATING SONG

A bracing breeze and a cloudless sky,
A rippling sea around us,
And o'er the waves my boat and I
Speed swift and sure as the sea birds fly,
Through the golden sheen
And the glistening gleam
Of the sunbeams that surround us.

A smiling path o'er the sparkling seas,
A compass true to guide us,
And gaily speeds my white-winged skiff
To the song of birds, and the balmy whiff
Of the perfumed breeze
From the sapphire seas
'Yond the waves that dance beside us.

A golden clime and a cloudless sky,
A calm, clear sea around us,
And peacefully my boat and I
Beside the land at anchor lie,
Our white sails furled
By the shores impearled
Of the beauteous land we found us.

May Carrol
P.E.I. Magazine
Vol. 1, #4

SHIPBUILDING

Shipbuilding flourished in Prince Edward Island for many years; indeed, it is still a small part of our economy in both small and large vessels. There were all types of sailing vessels of wooden construction in the early days, ranging from smacks, tugs, ferries and fishing boats. The period between 1840 and 1887 became known as the golden age of ship construction, with over 3,000 vessels launched.

The industry gave employment to thousands of men: shipwrights, carpenters, sailmakers, chandlers, blacksmiths, riggers and sparemakers in days past. The timber was usually cut in the winter and hauled out of the woods by a team of horses. Saws ripped logs into planks which were then placed in a steambox to soften them. Juniper and spruce were used for planking the frame and the deck. Pine wood made the best masts and spars. After launching, the vessels were loaded with farm produce and sailed to foreign ports of Great Britain, the West Indies, and the U.S.A. In many cases the ships were sold abroad.

In 1864 there were 50 shipbuilders with shipyards adjacent to a body of water deep and wide enough to accommodate the new vessel. The land gradually sloped down to the waters edge for easy launching. The best year of shipbuilding on P.E.I. was 1866 when there was 127 vessels built, averaging 243 tons. After 1875, the shipbuilding industry declined because of the invention of the steam engine and the depletion of the forests. Many Islanders were out of work and had to go off Island for employment.

Garden of the Gulf Museum

Ship building has not completely stopped. Our fishing boats are sold to far locations and our workers are currently contributing to the construction of larger vessels for the Canadian Armed Forces. Here are a few examples of production:

1781-1800: 93 vessels built with a total tonnage of 3,985 tonnes
1801-1810: 73 vessels built with a total tonnage of 4,984 tonnes
1811-1820: 238 vessels built with a total tonnage of 18,499 tonnes
1873-(Confederation Year): 58 vessels were built with a total tonnage of 15,376 tonnes
1901-1947: 86 vessels built with a total tonnage of 4,426 tonnes.

In August of 1983, four Inuit residents of northern Quebec took possession of a used fishing boat in Alberton prior to sailing it home. They will use it for hunting, fishing and tourists. A number of Northport-built boats have gone north over the years. The Gallien boat shop in Northport has orders for seven-metre fibreglass boats that will be going north.

COMMON TERMINOLOGY

In the Spring-Summer, 1978 issue of *The Island Magazine*, Lewis R. Fishcher wrote about the Island shipping industry of the 19th century. He described several of the common terms used to describe vessels:

Barque: A vessel with three (or more) masts with square sails on the fore and main masts, and fore and aft sails on the after mast; generally 250-700 ton capacity.

Barquentine: A vessel with three (or more) masts with square sails on the foremast, and fore and aft sails on the main and after masts; generally in the 250-500 ton class.

Brig: A vessel with two masts with square sails on each; normally 150-300 ton capacity.

Brigantine: A vessel with two masts, carrying square sails on the foremast, and fore and aft sails on the main mast; generally 100-250 ton capacity, although some Island-built vessels exceeded 400 tons.

Schooner: A vessel with two (or more) masts, with fore and aft sails on both masts; generally less than 150 tons, although some of the three-masted schooners constructed on the Island in the early 1880s exceeded 700 tons.

Shallop: As used on the Island, this term referred to a vessel with one mast carrying fore and aft sails; generally less than 25 tons.

Ship: A vessel with three (or more) masts with square sails on each; the largest sailing vessel, almost always exceeding 500 tons.

Sloop: A vessel with a single mast, fore and aft rigged; generally less than 25 tons.

Tonnage: Used as a measurement of the carrying capacity of a vessel.

IN SOURIS WATERS

Fishermen report a number of wrecks just off-shore at Souris. Fishing nets get tangled and at least one anchor has been hauled up. Most are not identified, but one, the *Genevieve Ethel* is reported to lie in about 17 fathoms of water south of the Souris Light. The Newfoundland-built rum-runner was later used to fish herring and it is said a particularly good catch overloaded the boat and was the cause of her demise.

East along the shore, the *Sondry North* struck Shallop Rock. Even today wreckage occasionally works its way up through the sand, especially after a storm. In December 1962, the wooden vessel *Gloria May*, once of the Souris Dragger Fleet, was lost in a storm.

The *Arvanda*, *Helen Mar* and *Gypsy Bride* all reportedly sank in the area during the 1800s.

ANCHORS REMINDERS OF THE PAST

Anyone doubting the number of shipwrecks that surround the Island, only has to talk to divers and fishermen to ascertain just how much evidence remains even today. One of the most noticeable are anchors which are often found by fishermen, who snag their nets, or lobster trap lines on them.

Paul Murray found one in seven fathoms of water between his home port and East Point, which was estimated to be about 200 years old and possibly from the French fleet.

Captain Alvin Gunn and four others found a 10-foot anchor, so thickly covered in stones, shells and seaweed that visible markings could not be seen. The anchor hooked on to the purse line of the mackerel seine. When they began hauling the ropes, the 2,000-pound weight could only be handled with a hydraulic winch on board the vessel.. This, too, was estimated to be 200 years old.

Throughout this book you will find other references to anchors and shipwrecks. And, when driving around the Island, particularly on the shore roads, you will see them in yards, or on view at historic sites or museums.

ACKNOWLEDGEMENTS

A book of this kind is dependent on the research and dedication to history of many individuals. Their love and respect for the past has been the driving force behind the establishment of museums, writing of articles and books, donation of important papers to archives and the maintenance of materials from the past. And of course they deserve the most credit for sharing their knowledge with people like me. Frankly, this book could never have been written without the work of dozens of people and I thank them for it. It is impossible to name everyone, to even know what their names are. Some are acknowledged below; others will hopefully understand that I may have forgotten to include them, but I still appreciate their contribution. To explain just how these people contribute, I'm going to tell you about one grand lady of preservation.

Eileen Oulton, 1911-1978, wanted to get everything on paper so she took her wonderful collection of historic material and used it to found the Alberton Museum. She brought the old courthouse for $1 and it is now a National Historical Preservation Foundation. Thanks to the foresight and dedication of Ms. Oulton, the Alberton Museum is one of the richest sources of information in the province. Small it might be, but ask any question and the staff will do their utmost to help you. There are several other community museums in the province where you meet the same friendliness and enthusiasm for what you are doing. Among the treasures I found at the Alberton Museum was a listing of shipping casualties from 1896 to 1970 — page after page of simple listings. This is the type of material that was the foundation of *Shipwrecks and Seafaring Tales.*

Credits:

Those Were The Days — History of the North Side of the Boughton River

Mike Appleton of Charlottetown

Public Archives of Prince Edward Island

Lorne Johnston of Montague, the Ole Salt who got me hooked on seafaring tales

Walter O'Brien, a good buddy from days working at the *Guardian*

Sources:

Skye Pioneers and "The Island" by Malcolm A. MacQueen

The Guardian newspaper

Atlantic Diver Guide: Volume III Prince Edward Island and the

Magdalene Islands
Maritime Mysteries by Roland H. Sherwood
More Recollections of an Ole Salt by Lorne Johnston
The Story of Prince Edward Island by P. Blakeley and M. Vernon
Dr. Geoff Robinson
Our Island Story — broadcasts given over CFCY Charlottetown in the winter of 1948 by Carrie Ellen Holman
Atlantic Fisherman
Dr. T.W. Stewart, whose notes from Island newspapers at the Prince Edward Island Public and Legislative Library in Charlottetown were presented to the Dominion Archives by H.R. Stewart in 1966 and are now available through the P.E.I. Public Archives
Debbie Gamble Arsenault

Suggested Reading:
It Came By The Boat Load by Geoff and Dorothy Robinson (rum-running)
Nellie J. Banks by Geoff and Dorothy Robinson (rum-running)
Atlantic Diver Guide: Volume III Prince Edward Island and the Magdalene Islands by David N. Barron ISBN 0-9693141-2-4
Recollection of an Ole Salt and *More Recollection of an Ole Salt* by Lorne Johnston
The World of the Onedin Line by Alison McLeay, published by Douglas, David & Charles Limited, Vancouver, B.C.

Suggested Places to Visit:
Basin Head Fisheries Museum
West Point Lighthouse Museum
Alberton Museum
Public Archives of Prince Edward Island
Garden of the Gulf Museum

INDEX

(Vessel listings are by complete name, thus the *Emma M. Vickerson* (in italics), will be found under "E" and the *C.E. Haskell* under "C". People are listed by last name first.)